"Looking at the pages of this striking book filled with
Andrea Fazzari's beautiful photography and insightful
words, I inhaled the aroma of a fascinating culture
as if I were actually on a journey through Tokyo. Its
chefs, although young, are mature beyond their years,
constantly offering extraordinary emotion to the world.
Buon viaggio!"

MASSIMILIANO ALAJMO
Chef, Le Calandre, Padova, Italy

"I love Tokyo. It has one of the very best dining scenes
in the world, and I have been fortunate to eat in many
of the featured restaurants. I am a true fan of Andrea's
work; she is an exceptionally talented photographer.
Due to her utilization of natural light, she gives each
picture so much appeal and a true storytelling quality.
Tokyo New Wave is an amazing work of art that will not
only appeal to chefs and foodies, but also to travelers
and all those who admire beauty."

RICHARD EKKEBUS
Chef, Amber at The Landmark Mandarin Oriental,
Hong Kong

TOKYO
new wave

TOKYO
new wave

**31 CHEFS DEFINING JAPAN'S
NEXT GENERATION, WITH RECIPES**

ANDREA FAZZARI

TEN SPEED PRESS
California | New York

Published in the United States by Ten Speed Press, an imprint of the Crown
Publishing Group, a division of Penguin Random House LLC, New York.
www.crownpublishing.com
www.tenspeed.com

Ten Speed Press and the Ten Speed Press colophon are registered
trademarks of Penguin Random House LLC.

Library of Congress Cataloging-in-Publication Data
   Names: Fazzari, Andrea, author.
   Title: Tokyo new wave : 31 chefs defining Japan's next generation,
      with recipes / Andrea Fazzari.
   Description: First edition. | California : Ten Speed Press, 2018. | Includes
      bibliographical references and index.
   Identifiers: LCCN 2017024763 (print) | LCCN 2017029051 (ebook)
   Subjects: LCSH: Restaurants—Japan—Tokyo. | Cooks—Japan—Tokyo—
      Interviews. | Cooking, Japanese. | BISAC: COOKING / Regional & Ethnic /
      Japanese. | TRAVEL / Asia / Japan. | LCGFT: Cookbooks.
   Classification: LCC TX907.5.J32 (ebook) | LCC TX907.5.J32 T654 2018
      (print) | DDC 641.5952/135—dc23
   LC record available at https://lccn.loc.gov/2017024763

Hardcover ISBN: 978-0-399-57912-7
eBook ISBN: 978-0-399-57913-4

Printed in China

Design by Betsy Stromberg and Andrea Fazzari, based on a design
by Margaux Keres

10 9 8 7 6 5 4 3 2 1

First Edition

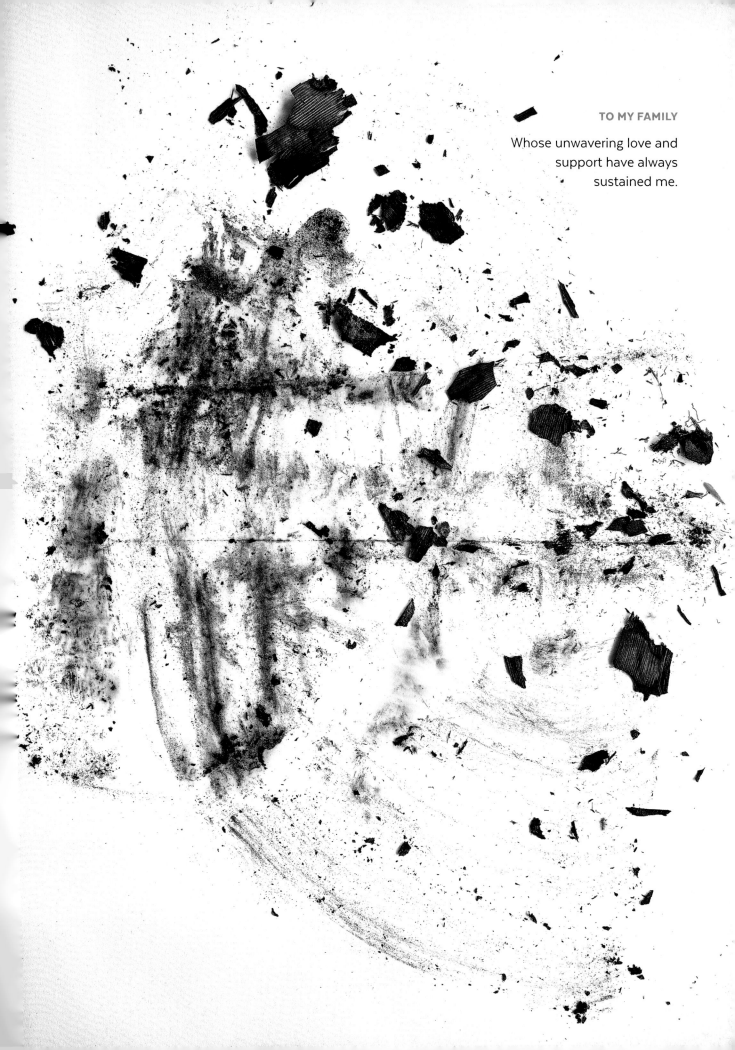

CONTENTS

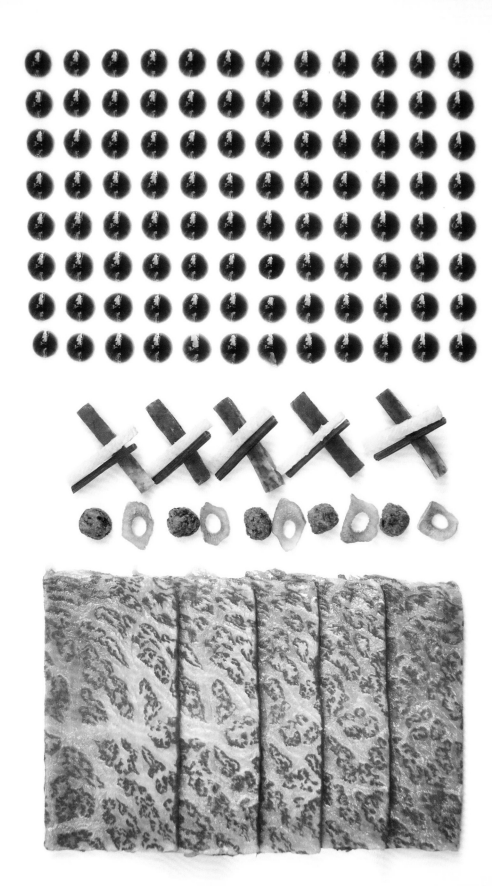

INTRODUCTION

Above all, this is a book of portraits, visual and written, of thirty-one chefs: thirty men and one woman.

It is a book about personality, identity, feeling, emotion, food, and Japan itself.

These chefs share their lives, their city, their country, and their humanity with me through the medium of food. Dining at their restaurants is never just about food; it is an accumulation of countless aspects that come together in the final expression on the plate, in hospitality, in service, in decor.

Food is at the center of culture—inherent in it is ceremony, politics, health, tradition, art, pleasure, satiation, agriculture, storytelling, and science. It is life itself. For many of these chefs, this is the first time they are part of a book, the first time they are even photographed or written about in this way, let alone by a foreigner. I am privileged to learn about these people, and privileged to spend time with them. I feel a great sense of honor and responsibility. This project is personal and has filled me with emotion, as does Japan itself.

In a country where craftsmanship, hospitality, and attention to detail are an art form, it is here in Tokyo that I feel drawn; it is here that I feel compelled to live, learn, explore, and understand. Both tradition and innovation are alive and well here, and it is this mix that is utterly compelling and vibrant.

Many in this newest generation of established Tokyo chefs are quite different in their attitudes and approach to dining than chefs were just ten years ago; as a group, they are much more open and less strict or mysterious than their predecessors. Japan is still a country not only deeply entrenched in local culinary tradition, but also fascinatingly influenced by other cultures, perhaps more so now than ever. A good number of the chefs have lived abroad and are as consumed with social media as people are everywhere else; they are curious, ambitious, funny, warm, exacting, confident, sometimes complicated, and unsure.

Some of the chefs are good friends, and if not, they at least know of each other, as they are part of a rather small community within a vast city. Their precision and pride, their sense of honor and dedication to their craft, their grace and the manner in which they manifest who they are and what it means to be Japanese, is, to me, an unparalleled way of existing in the world. Any chef who has never been to Japan, anyone who is fascinated by food but who has never been to Japan, is simply missing out. He or she is unknowingly unaware of a whole universe that embodies the epitome of gastronomy, where the array of flavors, of techniques, of ideas, and of ways of cooking, thinking, and behaving, are on some other sublime plane separate from the rest of the planet. I came to live here amid all of this, amid all the countless details, in appreciation of the millions of people who notice and value them as much as I do. Through its chefs I am learning about Japan and understanding how life is defined here. It is an intoxicating, magical, and enigmatic journey of exhilarating discovery. Although I accept that I can never and will never fully understand most of what it means to be Japanese even if I were to live here for a lifetime, I am swept up in its way of being, in its extraordinary style and approach to life, and its unique relationship with food.

ZAIYU
HASEGAWA

DEN

HAPPINESS

HOSPITALITY

Years ago in São Paulo, I photographed the influential Brazilian chef Alex Atala. I began to follow Atala on Instagram and noticed a post of a guest Japanese chef at Atala's restaurant, D.O.M. His name was Zaiyu Hasegawa. He was captivating, with wide cheekbones, a shock of shiny, spiked, gelled hair, and a large beauty mark dotting his right cheek. In all the photographs he was gregarious, with a magnetic energy. I vowed to visit his restaurant, Den, in Tokyo.

One year later, I move to Tokyo and have a coveted dinner reservation at Den, in Jimbocho, the night I arrive. For the first seating, I am welcomed and escorted to the center of the counter, directly in front of Hasegawa in his galley kitchen. He is exactly as I remember, but no longer just a one-dimensional photograph on my iPhone. While cooking, he chats and jokes with his guests at the counter, pausing to relish our reactions to each of his dishes. This chef, this hospitality, and this extraordinarily unique meal plunge me into Tokyo's culinary world.

The *omakase*-only (chef's choice) dinners at Den are not only culinary adventures, but also a joyful, new way of experiencing *nihon ryori* (Japanese cooking). Tokyo-born Hasegawa has a blast sharing his hospitality; he loves that I am a guest at his restaurant, and is eager to elicit smiles and laughs. His famous stuffed Dentucky Fried Chicken wing arrives in a cardboard box personalized with gifts. My box contains a mini American flag, a yellow rubber ducky, and a hand-drawn sign exclaiming "welcome!" There are whimsical smiley-face carrots in my twenty-two-ingredient salad, along with boiled ants from Chiba atop cooked root vegetables. This individualized and humorous presentation reflects Hasegawa's mischievous, original flair, and his infectiously happy personality.

Noriko Yamaguchi, Hasegawa's head of service, provides detailed context about each course and ingredient. She answers all of my questions about the stunning ceramics and flavors with ease and care. Noriko is one of the members of Team Den—which also includes Keiichi Terada, Rei Mochizuki (one of the few female sous chefs in Tokyo), and French pastry chef Remi Talbot. Emi, Hasegawa's wife and business partner, is a welcoming and radiant host; her kindness and warmth are at the soul of Den. And Puchi Sr., Hasegawa's beloved black-and-white Chihuahua, has been his constant companion in life. Once the memorable meal has ended, Hasegawa and Team Den all follow me outside to wave goodbye.

Thirty-nine-year-old Hasegawa is an undisputed leader of this current generation of Tokyo chefs. His brand of innovation is singular, and his playful, heartfelt style of *omotenashi* (the art of selfless hospitality) is a unique gift. Hasegawa personifies *genki*—a Japanese word meaning spirited, energetic, vivacious—and his profound culinary skills and knowledge of *nihon ryori* are impressive, winning him global praise and a coveted spot on the World's 50 Best list. It is not an understatement to say that Hasegawa is revered, even beloved.

Now, years later, Den has moved to a new location in Jingumae, and Puchi Jr., Hasegawa's brown-and-white long-haired Chihuahua, is the adored mascot. I continue to visit at least once a month, and am ceaselessly moved by a profound feeling of friendship through food, an unwavering sense that I am home.

OPPOSITE (clockwise from upper left): Noriko Yamaguchi, Den's head of service; Emi Hasegawa; chefs Susumu Shimizu (page 163), Hiroyasu Kawate (page 15), and Hasegawa; Rei Mochizuki, Den's sous chef.

INTER VIEW

Zaiyu is a unique name. What is its origin?

One of my relatives is a Buddhist priest, and he named me Zaiyu, which means "to do good things and to help others." When Japanese Buddhists pass away, they receive a new name for the afterworld. In my case, I can use the same name in the afterworld because a priest gave me my name.

Why do you cook?

I love seeing people eat and enjoy my food. In my experience, there are a lot of nice places to eat, but I can never actually remember what I ate. I remember the restaurant more if it makes me feel something. So I wanted my own restaurant to give people a feeling, an experience.

Guests respond strongly to your welcoming style here at Den. Did you set out to develop a style of hospitality that feels like eating with family?

I grew up in a large family, but today's families are smaller. People care less about—and for—others. When I was a child, my family and neighbors tried to teach me about life and raise me. I treat my staff like family. I am always thinking about Team Den—if we are all well, if everyone is happy. My employees and customers are a part of an extended family.

What is your favorite place or town to visit in Japan and why?

I like going to the mountains in general, but specifically Fuji-san [Mount Fuji], so I can forage wild mushrooms.

What was your childhood like?

My mother was very hardworking. She was a geisha, and even when she worked late, she always prepared a nice meal for me and my siblings. I always felt taken care of. She made things like miso soup, gyoza, rice, hamburger, and even beef stroganoff.

Whenever I would see my mother dressed a geisha, she was a totally different person. She was transformed. She would not talk to me. I'm the second child, so I had to take care of my youngest brother and sister. Because of this, I cooked from a young age, making them fried rice, *nigiri* [a slice of fish over vinegared sushi rice], sandwiches, and Japanese spaghetti.

What is your earliest food memory?

My mother introduced me to *omiyage*, a kind of bento box that she would bring home from elaborate *kaiseki* (haute cuisine) meals. She would surprise us with these gorgeous, tasty little gifts when we woke up in the morning. It was so exciting! It was after eating one of these *omiyage* that I began to think about cooking as a profession. I was twelve or thirteen years old. By high school, I knew I wanted to be a chef.

For you, what does it mean to be Japanese?

I think that Japanese people consider and think about other people more. When Japanese people have a given goal, I think they try to assess how the decision will affect others in their lives. I also think that Japanese people are not good at being direct. There are good and bad aspects of being Japanese, and I realize that when I am in other countries I need to act a bit differently. If I say whatever is on my mind to just everyone, I'm afraid I will hurt people's feelings.

Do you have future plans or goals?

I do think about the future, especially for children. I hope children will think about becoming chefs. Now young people don't think about becoming chefs so much. For children in Japan, it's hard to go to Japanese restaurants. In the future, I'd like to create more opportunities for children to cook and learn about food in Japan.

What is your favorite word?

Fun.

UNI IN SOY BÉCHAMEL SAUCE

Uni *comes from the sea, while* yuba *comes from the soil. The idea behind this dish is to play on the creamy texture that they both share, despite coming from different sources.*

¼ cup soy sauce

¼ cup sake

¼ cup mirin

28 yellow or orange pieces of soft, creamy uni (sea urchin), at room temperature

8 dark yellow pieces of firm uni, at room temperature

3½ tablespoons unsalted butter

¼ cup flour

2 cups soy milk

1⅔ cups heavy cream

Sea salt

3 ounces fresh yuba sheets

Dab of freshly grated wasabi root or small ball of wasabi paste

SERVES 4

In a medium bowl, mix together the soy sauce, sake, and mirin. Add the two types of uni, toss gently, and marinate at room temperature for 5 minutes, then drain.

Melt the butter in a saucepan over low heat. Stir in the flour and continue to cook the mixture for about 10 minutes, until little bubbles appear. Add the soy milk, a little at a time, stirring constantly, so that no lumps form. Bring the mixture to a boil, stirring constantly with a whisk, until the mixture thickens and becomes glossy, about 5 minutes. Remove from the heat. Stir in the heavy cream and season with a pinch of salt.

To finish, cut the yuba into bite-size strips, place it in four serving bowls, and then pour the cream mixture over the yuba. Put seven soft uni in the center of the mixture. Place two pieces of the firm uni on top of each serving, and then garnish the uni with some wasabi. Serve right away.

NOTE: Fresh *yuba* sheets (also known as tofu skin) can be purchased at Japanese grocers. *Uni* comes packaged in a box, no cleaning needed, and can be found at high-end seafood markets and Japanese markets. Ask for the highest grade for this preparation and buy the freshest *uni* possible. If there is no expiration date, make sure the *uni* has bright color and is in nice plump lobes. *Uni* can vary in softness, and you will need one firm type and one softer type for this recipe. Ask your fishmonger for assistance.

HIROYASU
KAWATE

FLORILÈGE

MODERNITY

INSTINCT

The first time I arrive at Florilège, I feel a potent sense of excitement and possibility. It feels like a revelation. This is an event. The interior doesn't feel like any other—it is both uniquely Japanese and internationally urbane. A charcoal gray-and-black open space features two expansive islands that are the centerpiece of this modern, theaterlike setting. Hot pink-and-gray upholstered chairs dot the slate counter lit by spotlights. Watching boyish, tall, and down-to-earth Hiroyasu Kawate and his staff scurry around the impressive kitchen is beguiling, as is the plating—minimalist, assertive, and chic. Each ceramic dish is a statement in and of itself and elicits touch, adding to the interest and anticipation of each subsequent course. Some might call Kawate's food French Fusion or Japanese French, but I do not, as that would limit its breadth and essence. His cuisine evades labeling, existing in a new category of its own. An earthy refinement and clear confidence come through in Kawate's creations; eating here is about terroir, discovery, and a peek into the future of dining.

I return. Again, I feel the same exhilaration upon arrival. The energy and emotion Kawate communicates through his food, through his choice of pottery, through his sheer drive and frenzied exuberance, convey a refreshing, upbeat vitality. There is fried *ayu* and *ayu* ravioli with passion fruit, cream, caramel, peas, and pancetta (see photo, page 21); bonito with white clam and coffee sauce; beef with smoked potato puree, beet consommé, and parsley oil. Prawns with herb salad and lemon-butter crystals are served in a stunning deep gray-and-white glossy handmade bowl, the presentation arresting, colorful . . . and original. These dishes open a window into Kawate's mind, and reflect his deep bond with the farmers who harvest the products that stir his creativity. His accomplished sous chef, Tahara Ryogo, serves me with flair, describing each dish in Italian.

After another superlative meal one afternoon, Kawate emerges from the kitchen to say goodbye, and presents me with a small wrapped box. He would like to thank me for some photographs, and this time he hugs me, abandoning the usual bow. At home, I gingerly open the wooden box to find an exquisite bud vase made by one of his potters. I am touched by Kawate's thoughtfulness.

Two years later, I continue to dine frequently at Florilège, and still feel that sense of anticipation as I did on my first visit. The vase Kawate gave me remains a symbol of the warmth I have encountered here in Japan, the artisanal beauty that surrounds me, and the power of dining as much more than the food itself.

INTERVIEW

Why do you cook?

The food my mother made when I was growing up here in Tokyo was not special as far as technique, but it made people happy. I wanted to make that type of soulful food, just with more culinary technique. I like to tailor dishes to each person. I wanted an open a restaurant so I could talk with people and communicate through my dishes. Customers can feel my heart through my food. They want to taste this energy, taste this feeling.

What has the biggest influence on your cooking?

My father and cooking in his kitchen. He was a *yōshoku* cook [of Japanese-influenced Western food]. When I was little, I would do my homework in the kitchen on a small table while he was prepping. I wasn't allowed to help. It smelled really nice, and my dad looked very happy doing his work. I was able to learn a few things about cooking from my dad at home, but not at his restaurant.

What is your earliest food memory?

Japanese *hambāgu,* or hamburger steak. It's kind of like meat loaf. I remember the portions were always so big at home, more than Dad served at his restaurant—I felt so special. To this day, I love to eat it.

Who do you admire in the food world?

The farmers. There's one farmer named Shiro Fuji who has a small family farm, named Fuji Noen Saku, in Nagano. He grows many of my vegetables, like turnips, carrots, and tomatoes. There are many well-known farmers in Japan, but most of them don't think about the people who are actually eating their produce. This farmer does, and he wants to make the customers happy. All of my dishes are inspired by the farmers, hunters, and fishermen within our food culture.

Why did you decide on this striking and open design for the restaurant?

I definitely wanted to see diners eating and interact with them. I was inspired by the design of Atera in Manhattan and wanted to reinterpret what I saw there. For service, I was influenced by traditional Japanese counter service and it seemed quite natural that the cooks don't just make the dishes but serve them themselves.

For you, what does it mean to be Japanese?

That is a difficult question. I have never thought about what being Japanese really means. In a way, it is my identification with my family—but I feel that I could actually be from anywhere.

If you could share a meal with anyone, who would it be?

Sen no Rikyu, the legendary tea master who perfected the way of tea, or *chanoyu.*

Yuzan Kaibara, a character in the manga and TV series *Oishinbo* [*The Gourmet*].

My great-great-grandfather, who actually cooked for Emperor Meiji.

What cause or charity is most important to you?

Reducing food waste. It's a big problem in Japan and around the world. When I cook, I use the whole animal, and I keep vegetable scraps, using them in some other application. "One man's trash is another man's treasure."

What is your favorite word?

Freedom.

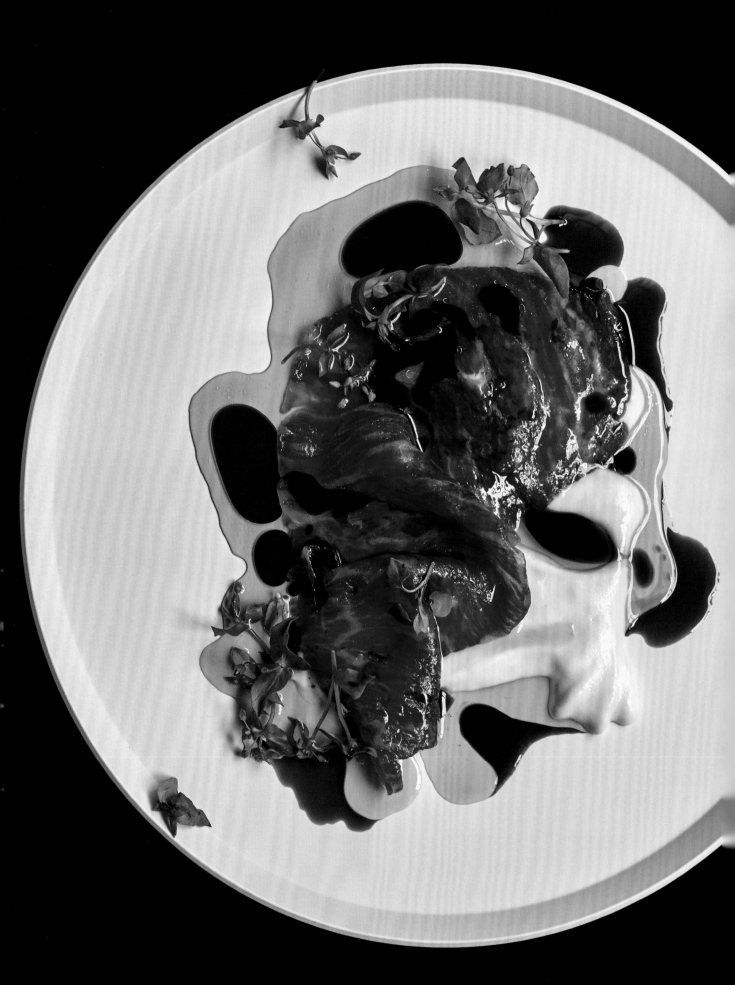

WAGYU CARPACCIO WITH POTATO PUREE AND BEET CONSOMMÉ

Beef and beets are foods that I have been familiar with since I staged in Montpellier, France. They are often on my mind as a great combination. I came up with this recipe using the special kind of beef that comes from an older Japanese dairy cow.

CARPACCIO

7 ounces Wagyu beef New York Strip

1 teaspoon sea salt

½ teaspoon sugar

BEET CONSOMMÉ

6 cups veal stock

12 ounces ground chuck roast

½ cup chopped white or yellow onion

½ cup chopped celery

½ cup chopped carrot

½ cup chopped beet

¼ cup chopped tomato

4 egg whites

1 tarragon sprig

1 thyme sprig

POTATO PUREE

8 ounces russet potatoes, peeled and cut into chunks

1 cup milk

1 cup heavy cream

½ teaspoon sea salt

PARSLEY OIL

½ cup minced fresh parsley

⅔ cup sunflower oil

Micro chervil leaves, for garnish

SERVES 4

To prepare the carpaccio, trim the beef of any fat and cut into four ¼-inch-thick lengthwise slices. One by one, cover a beef slice with plastic wrap and pound with a meat mallet or the bottom of a heavy pan until paper-thin. Sprinkle the salt and sugar on both sides of the flattened beef slices and transfer to a metal wire rack so that air can circulate and dry the meat. Refrigerate uncovered for 6 hours to dry the beef.

To make the consommé, warm the stock in a saucepan until it's 105°F or quite hot to the touch, like a Jacuzzi. In a separate pot, combine the ground chuck roast, onion, celery, carrot, beet, and tomato and mix well by hand. Add the egg whites to the beef mixture, drizzling in a steady flow. Place over low heat and then add the warmed stock, a little at time, stirring constantly with a wooden spatula, until it gets close to a simmer. Stop stirring just before it is about to boil, then lower the heat, add the tarragon and thyme, and simmer until the stock is clear, about 1 hour. Strain through a fine-mesh sieve into a pot and keep warm. Discard the solids.

To prepare the potato puree, combine all of the ingredients in a medium pot and bring to a boil over high heat. Lower to a simmer and cook the potatoes until soft (test with knife), about 25 minutes. Transfer half of the liquid and all of the potatoes to a blender while still hot, and puree until smooth, about 3 minutes. If the mixture is too thick and doesn't blend properly, add a bit more of the liquid. Strain the mixture through a chinois or fine-mesh sieve into a bowl. Keep warm.

To make the parsley oil, combine the parsley and sunflower oil in a blender and puree until smooth. Strain the mixture through a fine-mesh sieve into a bowl.

Spoon a portion of the potato puree onto a serving plate and place one slice of the carpaccio over the puree. Drizzle with some of the parsley oil, and then pour ¼ cup of the consommé over the top. Repeat with the remaining plates, garnish with the micro chervil, and serve right away.

NOTE: This recipe calls for veal stock, which is available at some artisan butcher shops, but you can also use good-quality beef stock.

PURPOSE

VISION

Occasionally, a chef is much more than his title. He reaches beyond his work in the kitchen to create something larger than his restaurant and even himself. Shinobu Namae, forty-three, is an advocate and cerebral adventurer who possesses a purposeful idealism, the belief that peace and harmony are attainable through food.

Traveling regularly both domestically and internationally, Yokohama-born Namae simultaneously embraces tradition and modernity. Within Japan, he visits craftsmen whose families have been making miso, soy sauce, bonito, and sake for generations. These are his *sensei*, from whom he learns about process and technique. They are a source of inspiration for him, as are numerous other purveyors and farmers whom Namae regards as his extended community. He thoughtfully posts his experiences on social media, such as the making of *katsuobushi* (fermented and smoked bonito); new designs from his favorite clothing designers, Matohu, who designed his staff's uniforms; a tea ceremony with his tea master, Soko Udagawa; and a visit from his revered mentor, Michel Bras. No one is excluded from sharing in his discoveries or his learning process, and that includes his large yet familial staff at his restaurant, L'Effervescence.

The Japanese tea ceremony is significant to Namae, so much so that it closes the dining experience at L'Effervescence, performed tableside by one of his staff . I accompany Namae to visit his tea master from whom he continually learns and practices the tea ceremony, contemplating both its inner and outer forms. What strikes me beyond the idyllic setting and mesmerizing intricacies of the master's movements is Namae's contentment. His serene pleasure in sharing the way of tea and his openness and generosity of spirit are evident here and in his imaginative dishes at L'Effervescence, such as Where the Ocean Meets the Land (venison sirloin with scallop mousseline, charred red pepper, and red shiso sauce) and his signature dish, A Fixed Point (a four-hour roasted turnip with brioche croutons, Basque ham, and parsley).

Namae's essential desire to innovate and look beyond the country of his birth fuels him; for Namae, borders are a political phenomenon, only limiting human experience and understanding. At L'Effervescence, culture, history, politics, science, and refinement are all present and all connected, in the space and on the plate. Namae is aware that his elegant restaurant's two Michelin stars and World's 50 Best Restaurants ranking are a magnet for many customers, yet these are neither his motivation nor his goal.

With his sharp focus and intense gaze, Namae affirms, "Nature is a part of me, and I am a part of nature." His search for knowledge, understanding, and harmony and his belief in the benevolent power of food will never end.

S. Namae

INTERVIEW

Why do you cook?

Cooking is not everything to me, but it is very important. Through cooking, I try to communicate with people. Restaurants can connect culture, lifestyle, and politics. We source our main products from local farmers and artisans, not from supermarkets where we don't know anything about the products. Our cooking, staff, servers—we are all connected and close. This is how the restaurant can be an example of contributing to a better society.

What inspires you?

When I cook, the seasons inspire me: the ingredients and flavors, the freshness, and the complexities of the seasons.

Beautiful scenery, like in Kyoto in the fall, inspires me. I see objects or things that are beautiful in and of themselves but they become more beautiful if I can share them and discuss them with someone, anyone. It can even be a stranger. I like to share ideas and feelings. It's all the same unless we share our perceptions of it. Feelings are individual. By sharing them with others through discussion, we can help define what it is or how beautiful it is.

Why did you become a chef?

Upon entering university, I had a part-time kitchen job in a casual Italian restaurant. The more I learned about Italian cooking, the more I wanted to learn about the country. When I graduated from university, I went to work in a popular Italian restaurant full-time. During these three years, I visited Italy twice and thought I wanted to be an Italian chef. Having grown up in Japan, Italian cuisine was easy for me to understand. French cuisine seemed too complicated and snobbish. I never liked it, and I hated French chefs.

Then what changed your mind?

In 2003, on a trip to New York City to learn new things about food, I found Kitchen Arts & Letters bookstore on the Upper East Side. When I opened the door, there was a shiny book on display—it was Michel Bras's book looking at me. When I saw it, I knew that this was what I was looking for. This was a different kind of cooking. I already had rough ideas for my own cooking style and wanted to respect the color and shape of all ingredients. The French chefs change things so much from the original form, which might be considered sophisticated, but it never resonated with me. This book touched me, I could see what things were. I didn't care about anything French until I saw this book. Everything was clear to me, and it felt like it was more like what I loved about Italian food.

OPPOSITE: The staff at L'Effervescence.

So this book changed your life?

This discovery, falling in love with this book in New York City, changed my life. I returned to Japan to ultimately work for Michel Bras in Hokkaido from 2003 to 2008. Those five years were everything for me. Then I spent a full year with Heston Blumenthal at Fat Duck in London, which was also quite valuable.

What is your earliest food memory?

I remember my mom's pretty bad miso soup in Yokohama. She made the broth out of anchovies and added handmade miso from Akita. Relatives always sent handmade miso to us, and it was rough and strong. Later, I went to a friend's home and loved their miso. My mom's wasn't good even though she was using good products. She created my palate with quality ingredients.

For you, what does it mean to be Japanese?

I identify myself not as Japanese but as a human being standing on this planet. Of course, I was born here in Japan and grew up here. But, my nationality doesn't matter to me; I could be from anywhere. I was raised Japanese, which influenced me—that's how I became who I am. But I don't need to be Japanese or the citizen of any particular country. I think this makes my cuisine more complicated.

How do you think growing up in Japan informs your style?

I think it does in physical ways, like my taste buds and palate, which have been influenced by Japanese flavors from childhood. I grew up with rice and wheat because after World War II, the U.S. government spread the consumption of wheat. When I was in elementary school, we had rice once a month and a buttered roll with jam. At home, I ate rice at dinner, but lots of bread at lunch at school. At breakfast, my mom would give us bread and British milled tea and sunny-side-up eggs every day.

If you could share a meal with anyone, who would it be?

Gandhi, no one else. His views of change and pacifism and reaching across castes and ethnicity to understand others is very inspiring to me. His character and desire to make the world a better place resonate with me.

Do you have a vision for your future?

It is the everyday accumulation that I believe is important, of making things better than yesterday.

I like unity, but I hate globalization. We are all different and shouldn't impose upon one another, but there has to be some imposition in order to understand and respect one another. This seems contradictory, and it is.

What is your favorite word?

Harmony.

L'EFFERVESCENCE TURNIP

The turnip conveys the season with its flavor, sweetness, and texture, which leads to an appreciation of the passage of time. With this recipe, my goal was also to reverse the usual ratio of meat to vegetables.

CROUTONS

¼ cup cubed brioche, cut into ⅛-inch cubes

PARSLEY OIL

½ cup flat-leaf parsley

1 teaspoon water

Sea salt

1 tablespoon sesame oil

TURNIP

1 medium turnip (6 ounces)

Fine sea salt

1 tablespoon sesame oil

2 tablespoons unsalted butter

¼ cup cubed semidried Bayonne or other cured ham, cut into ⅛-inch cubes

4 flat-leaf parsley leaves, for garnish

SERVES 1

To make the croutons, preheat the oven to 350°F. Spread the brioche cubes in a single layer on a baking sheet. Bake for 2 to 3 minutes, then turn the cubes over and bake for 7 to 8 minutes more, until light golden.

To make the parsley oil, put the parsley, water, a pinch of salt, and the sesame oil in a blender. Puree for 1 minute, until smooth. Pass through a fine-mesh sieve into a bowl, and set aside.

To make the turnip, cut off the greens and peel the turnip, removing the fibrous part between the outer layer and its core. Continue to pare down the turnip with a paring knife, maintaining its natural teardrop shape, until it weighs 2½ ounces. This will ensure it cooks correctly in the immersion cooker.

Rinse the turnip well and put it into a sous vide bag or a ziplock bag. Cook the turnip with an immersion circulator at 130°F to 165°F for 4 hours. Transfer the turnip in the bag to an ice bath to chill until cold, about 15 minutes.

Cut the turnip in half and season with sea salt. Warm the sesame oil in heavy pan over high heat. Place the turnip halves cut side down in the pan and sear for about 3 minutes, until light golden.

Add the butter and let it melt and sizzle. Continue to cook the turnip in the sizzling butter until the cut side turns deep brown and the butter begins to brown. Tilt the pan so the butter pools on one side, and using a tablespoon, pour the brown butter over the turnip repeatedly for 3 to 5 minutes, to make sure it is warmed through.

Paint a streak of parsley oil across the plate with a tablespoon. Place the croutons and ham in the center of the dish. Place the two cut sides of the turnip together and place on top of the croutons and ham. Sprinkle with the parsley leaves. Serve right away.

NOTE: You will need an immersion circulator or sous vide machine.

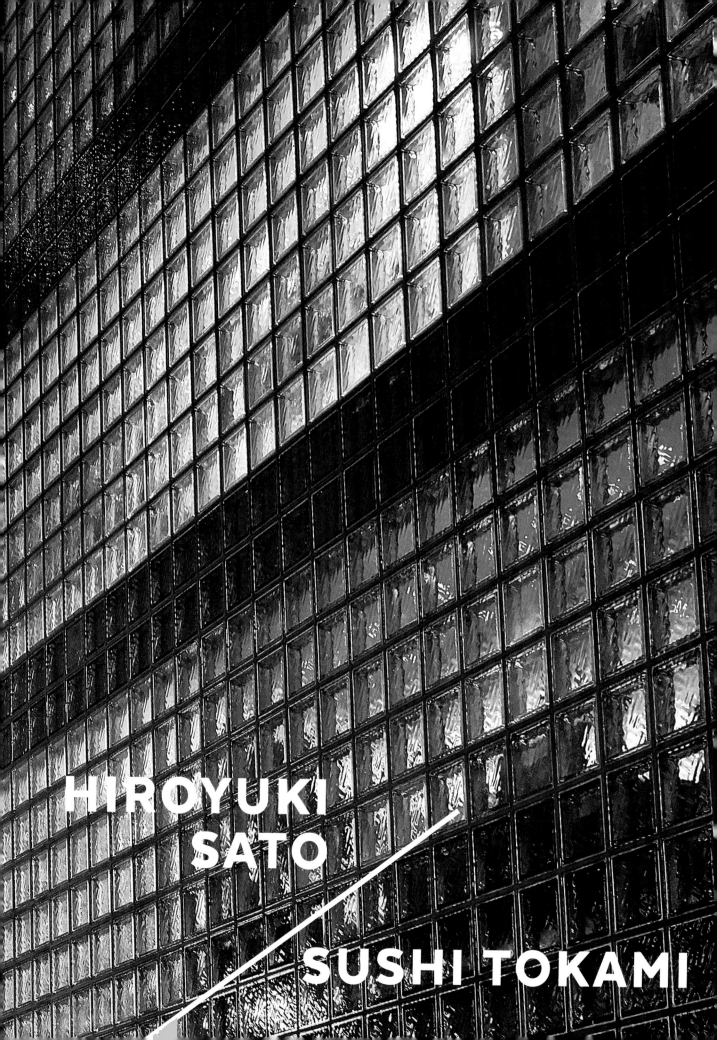

HIROYUKI
SATO

SUSHI TOKAMI

CALM

COOL

After lunch, the rigors of service completed, chef Hiroyuki Sato is relaxing and listening to Miles Davis on his iPhone. When I see him, I am struck by his appearance and extroverted demeanor. His high cheekbones and round features are heightened by his shaved head and luminous skin. Sato is simultaneously monastic and cool. He is relaxed and casual, exuding a calm and assured energy.

Sato is eager to speak English. He uses a translator app on his phone to supplement the simple sentences he already knows. After almost every sentence, he exclaims, "*So desu ne?*" (It is, isn't it?) with a nod and broad smile. His willingness to share and ask questions about me are indicative of his curiosity and openness. It is not common that a chef in Japan would be this inquisitive, especially during a first meeting.

He wants me to hear one of his favorite songs, the Boz Scaggs classic "We Are Not Alone." He tells me how much he loves this song, which he and his wife danced to at their wedding. We listen, as family meal—grilled fish, miso soup, and rice—is quietly prepared by his small staff of young men. He eats the fish and soup but forgoes the rice. "Why?" I ask. "I like to stay trim," he responds, patting his stomach.

A thirty-nine-year-old Tokyo native, Sato is known for his strong use of red sake lees vinegar in his rice. He chooses fish for its fat content and how it best suits the acidity of his vinegared rice. The rice is the star, he tells me, and the fish is chosen for it, not the other way around. Sushi is one of the most traditional of all the Japanese cuisines. The form, traditions, and methods of sushi are most certainly maintained and celebrated during service, but Sato himself is anything but traditional. He's also an avid surfer who spends a lot of time in the waters of Ibaraki Prefecture. Perhaps it is a stereotype to think of surfers as laid-back and easygoing, but Sato is, and he is as much at home on the beach as he is hosting Jodie Foster or Milla Jovovich at his Ginza sushi bar.

I subsequently meet Sato many times and our interactions are always uncomplicated and refreshingly lighthearted. He invites me to a barbecue to spend time with his friends and to meet his wife and two young boys. While grilling oysters, he reveals that he will not be a sushi chef forever, despite his Michelin star. "I just want to be happy and have a simple life."

INTERVIEW

When did you know you wanted to be a chef?

When I was twenty-five. I had been a waiter for a long time. Waiting tables is not really an admired job here in Japan. I liked creating. My father was a sushi chef, so I grew up knowing what a sushi chef was, but I never worked with him. He is still in Shinagawa at his own restaurant. If my dad had been a tempura chef, I would have become a tempura chef.

What type of sushi do you make?

I make Edo-style sushi. The rice vinegar most typically used in Edo-style sushi goes well with fatty fish but I do *not* use rice vinegar. Instead I use red vinegar made from *sake kasu*, or sake lees in English, left over after sake production, which pairs well with all kinds of fish, fatty or more lean. I like the umami and the body of it, how my vinegar interacts with the fish. Balance is also very important between the rice, the vinegar, and the fish. For me, the *shari* [flavored rice] is the most important thing. Many chefs match their rice to the fish, but I match my fish to the rice. I tailor what I make according to the customer. I observe everyone and try to intuit what they want from their energy. I can vary the amount of the vinegar and the size of the fish depending on the guest's height and weight. Even their mannerisms and the impression they give me can dictate what and how I serve them. This is not something unique to me; all sushi chefs do this.

What is your earliest food memory?

My mom's food. I remember eating udon when I was sick. It was not all from scratch, but always really, really good and delicious.

For you, what does it mean to be Japanese?

It's hard to say exactly. I know that when I go overseas I miss Japan a lot. It's definitely something I feel. For me, much of what it means to be Japanese is sushi. I want to travel internationally to teach more people about what real sushi is. I enjoy doing this a great deal, sharing how it is made and showing people an aspect of Japanese culture.

If you could share a meal with anyone, who would it be?

My great-grandparents and my great-great-grandparents.

Duke Kahanamoku, a Hawaiian surfer who lived from 1890 to 1968.

What is your favorite word?

Happiness.

What is a favorite film of yours and why?

The Shawshank Redemption. I really like the theme of strong friendship, trust, and dedication.

YOSUKE
SUGA

SUGALABO

DRIVE

LUXURY

I once had dinner at L'Atelier de Joël Robuchon at the Four Seasons Hotel in New York City when Yosuke Suga was the head chef. Ten years later, I am zipping around Tokyo with him in his silver Porsche Carrera. Jazz is playing. It is about 6:30 p.m. and there is traffic in Omotesando driving toward Shinjuku.

Suga is focused and ambitious—very ambitious. He is driven to be the best and will admit to as much. During a sixteen-year stint working for Joël Robuchon, he lived in both Paris and New York City. His introduction-only restaurant, Sugalabo, in Azabudai, is a success, as is a booming catering business for luxury brands. Suga is a multitasker who is focused on his desire to do more, create more, be more. His urbane and refined sensibility is front and center.

The secret entrance to Sugalabo lies behind a camouflaged door in a coffee bar. By day, it is a tiny kiosk manned by just one staff member who sells housemade madeleines and coffee. By night, it becomes the foyer to an exclusive dinner club. On my first visit in December, I feel along a wall to find a handle. I push it and enter an elegant kitchen—the restaurant itself. It is a hushed and luxurious speakeasy sparkling with copious hanging brass pots, flickering gas candlelight, and crackling fireplaces.

Suga personally presents every course, explaining the provenance of each ingredient and the concept behind each dish. He speaks purposefully, frowning, deliberating every word before it exits his mouth. He commands the room with an eaglelike precision; nothing that is done or not done escapes his notice.

At the front of the restaurant, framed photos of Suga's grandfather are displayed atop shelves of culinary books. There is a distinct resemblance between Suga and the man in the maritime black-and-white photos. His grandfather was a European cuisine chef aboard a luxury ship, and has long been a source of inspiration for Suga—a compass, a point of reference. When Suga speaks of his grandfather, I sense a tinge of melancholy, perhaps a bit of longing.

Suga often travels throughout Japan discovering new products and deepening relationships with farmers and purveyors. This mission, this immersion into Japan, is part of Suga's identity. Despite having lived abroad for many years and a love for far-flung places, or perhaps because of it, he is drawn, from deep within his soul, to live in Japan now. It is where he feels most deeply connected. This comes across when dining at Sugalabo, where these themes of identity, of longing, of beauty, and of discovery are presented in Suga's way, with both love and luxury.

INTERVIEW

Why do you cook?

So I can express myself. I like to express my savoir faire. I like restaurants; they're not only about food. They're to make people feel pleasure. Everything I do now is so I can find something to do that is exciting. Life is only lived once; I don't want it to be boring.

Also, the memory of my grandfather motivates me. I think my family is the most important thing in my life. I like to bring pleasure to my guests, but originally, all of this was to bring pleasure to my family. An homage to my grandfather brings pleasure to my father. I don't have a lot of memories of my grandfather—I didn't have his food when he was alive, cooked by him. But I have lots of memories in my father's restaurant where they cooked my grandfather's recipes. My grandfather cooked yōshoku [Western food adapted to Japanese taste] with a bit of French influence. That was many years ago, at the time when products like foie gras were not available here yet. At the time, it was impossible to do real French food, but he did and was avant-garde at the time. It was the Belle Époque—the time of Charlie Chaplin, Helen Keller. They were actually guests on the luxury ship that he worked on, which sailed from Kobe to San Francisco. He cooked for them.

Why did you want to leave Japan?

So I could have an expanded culinary and life experience. At twenty-one years old, I was still young. I knew I had a lot to learn. I could get complacent without a master. I wanted to go to France because I am romantic, like many chefs who cook French food. The nuances in Japanese culture are very different than those in France or Italy. People here dream of living in France and Italy. I was realistic but romantic and wanted to go to France to be different; I wanted to discover real French cuisine in France with Robuchon at his small laboratory. Only two or three chefs worked for him. I had a special opportunity.

Tell me about Joël Robuchon.

I started working with him when I was twenty-one years old. He was considered one of the very best chefs in the world. Even chef of the century. At age forty-nine, he had already retired and closed his fine dining restaurant, Joël Robuchon, in the 16th arrondissement in Paris to open his laboratory, a place where chefs could experiment and devise new recipes. I worked with him there and on his French television show.

Then, at age sixty, Robuchon decided to open restaurants again, starting with L'Atelier de Joël Robuchon in various cities. The Ateliers had a huge counter, tapas-style, with the look of a sushi counter and an open kitchen, which is rare in Europe but popular in Japan. I came to Roppongi Hills by myself at twenty-four to open Tokyo's L'Atelier de Joël Robuchon. I then opened others, and stayed with him until I was thirty-seven years old.

How are you different from other chefs?

I am a bit more independent. I have a different vision of what a restaurant should be and the possibilities of food and restaurants. Stars and rankings are not my goal. I don't like being classified or branded by others. I think it's important to be independent and respected, and to have my own approach to my branding.

What is your earliest food memory?

My grandfather was already gone, but my dad kept his restaurant, Kobe-ya, in Nagoya. I remember always sitting in the corner there with a little stuffed animal and I would have sautéed pork with ginger sauce and beef stroganoff.

For you, what does it mean to be Japanese?

Morals. Character. My respect for the trees and the flowers and the seasons—it's part of the spirit of Japan. Shintoism. Gods in everything. I also respect many religions.

I am not typically Japanese. I am not timid. I am a bit aggressive. I am perhaps an optimist. I am open and can be assertive. I also have aFrench side. I am a realist. I am pretty direct.

How is this reflected in your food?

The ingredients, most of which are from Japan. In Japanese culture, if you use Japanese ingredients that are seasonal, from this particular geography, it means cooking more and more deeply in the style of Japanese cuisine. Sea bass, for example, is different in each country. Just as good, but different. When you cook it here, the sea bass texture is different. You have to think about and consider the products and how they react and behave. Then it becomes less French and more Japanese. You must understand local ingredients.

Do you have a specific goal for the future?

Right now, I don't think there is anyone in the culinary world who translates and presents Japanese food culture abroad, as it should be presented. One day I would like to be a kind of ambassador bringing foreigners, and also Japanese, to the many regions of Japan. So many young people live in the big cities exclusively. I would like to bring more people to small villages and farms to discover the traditions of Japanese food culture. I also came back to Japan to do something different from others chefs. I would like to open a restaurant abroad, but I want this to be my base now.

What is your favorite word?

Voyage.

KONATSU LEMONGRASS SORBET

Konatsu, a grapefruitlike citrus, was in season when I came up with this recipe. I was traveling in Kochi with Shiraki-san, the farmer. I walked around his farm with him; his product is beautiful. The dessert is light after the meal, and I like the name. Coconuts and konatsu are similar in sound and also work well together.

CITRUS FRUIT SYRUP

1¼ cups water

5 tablespoons granulated sugar

2 tablespoons glucose syrup

1½ lemongrass stalks, chopped

½ vanilla bean, split lengthwise and scraped with a knife

1 star anise

1 strip orange zest

1 strip lemon zest

COCO-LYCHEE SORBET

½ cup plus 1 tablespoon water

¼ cup granulated sugar

2 teaspoons glucose syrup

2 teaspoons trimoline

⅓ teaspoon ice cream stabilizer

1 cup frozen coconut puree

1 tablespoon Dita (lychee liqueur)

KONATSU CONFIT AND KONATSU CHIPS

10 whole frozen konatsu or fresh oranges, or 5 grapefruits

½ cup granulated sugar

⅓ cup plus 1 tablespoon water

Confectioners' sugar, to sprinkle

10 lychees, peeled, pitted, and halved

5 tablespoons small flakes of gold foil, for garnish

SERVES 20

To make the syrup, combine the water, granulated sugar, and glucose syrup in a small saucepan and bring to a boil. Remove from the heat. Add the lemongrass, vanilla seeds and pod, star anise, orange zest, and lemon zest. Let infuse for 20 minutes. Strain through a fine-mesh sieve into a bowl and let cool. Discard the solids.

To make the sorbet, combine the water, granulated sugar, glucose syrup, and trimoline in a pot and cook over medium heat. Before it reaches a boil (do not allow it to come to a boil), remove from the heat, add the ice cream stabilizer, and mix well. Let cool, then add the coconut puree and stir. Add the Dita and stir again. Freeze sorbet in an ice cream maker for 20 minutes.

To make the konatsu confit, peel the rind from half of the konatsu and julienne. Combine the granulated sugar and water in a pot and bring to a simmer over medium-low heat. Add the julienned rind and simmer until the peel becomes transparent, 30 to 40 minutes. Drain and let cool.

To make the konatsu chips, preheat a convection oven to 165°F or a regular oven to 200°F. Peel the remaining konatsu and remove any zest from the fruit. Cut each konatsu in half, then into thick slices. Arrange on baking sheets in a single layer and sprinkle with confectioners' sugar. Bake until completely crystallized and dried out, about 2 hours with a convection oven, 4 hours with a regular oven.

For each serving, place 1 tablespoon of the syrup, three pieces of the konatsu confit, and half of a lychee in a glass bowl. Shape 1 heaping tablespoon of the sorbet into a quenelle and place on top. Top with one konatsu chip and sprinkle with ¼ teaspoon gold foil flakes. Serve right away.

NOTE: *Konatsu* comes frozen in Japan, but you can use fresh grapefruit or orange instead. You can buy a canned ice cream stabilizer on some cooking sites; otherwise, substitute with cornstarch, guar gum, arrowroot, or carrageenan (but all have mixed results). Coconut puree is available on Amazon and other online stores.

KOJI
KOIZUMI

KOHAKU

GRACE

POETRY

Koji Koizumi is a modern-day culinary version of the legendary film director Yasujiro Ozu. Ozu revered the seasonality of life. His films tell the stories of families in postwar Japan in long unedited takes; they are unhurried, and observant of the smallest details of quotidian Japanese life. As integral as his characters are to these films, nature and the seasons are just as or perhaps even more significant. Ozu's films, such as *Early Spring* and *Late Fall*, illustrate the Japanese culture's deep-seated, visceral connection to nature and the seasons.

At thirty-seven years old, Koizumi's culinary style is guided by twenty-four microseasons. As we sit and chat in his light, airy, and sophisticated dining room at Kohaku, in the former geisha district of Kagurazaka, he tells me about the significance of the seasons to his life, cooking, and vision. We discuss Shintoism, Buddhism, and how lives in Japan are generally imbued with a rhythm and significance dictated by nature. It is simultaneously a teacher, a guiding force, and an inspiration.

Koizumi's restaurant, Kohaku, is a showcase for the artistry and spirit of *kaiseki* cuisine (haute cuisine)—a confluence of the seasons, the farmers and artisans who make the ingredients, and the beliefs in the health benefits of food—steeped in abundant, profound symbolism. Every choice at this three-Michelin-starred restaurant is made with profound intention and consideration. With great eagerness, Koizumi is content to expound upon the philosophy of Kohaku, and themes of connectedness and nature.

Koizumi's *shisho* (master) is Hideki Ishikawa, the renowned, revered, and humble *kaiseki* chef, who Koizumi trained with for eight years. What differentiates Koizumi from Ishikawa is Koizumi's use of fine ingredients from around the world (his mentor uses exclusively Japanese ingredients), the way he creates his *omakase* (chef's choice) menu with these ingredients, and a more modern dining space. The beauty of Kohaku is that it is both traditional and contemporary—I can see the past and the future of Japan.

It is late summer when I photograph Koizumi. As I am shooting, I ask him with whom he would like to dine given the chance. He reveals that he would like to have dinner with himself in another life, before he was born and reincarnated as the person he is today. This answer has stayed with me, both thoughtful and sensitive, traditionally and contemporarily Japanese.

INTERVIEW

What does *kaiseki* cuisine—and your cuisine, in particular—illustrate about Japan?

In *kaiseki*, there are a lot of craftsmen and artisans behind everything. There's the presentation, the person serving—it's the gathering of many people's spirits.

Seasons are very important to me and to most Japanese chefs. The ingredients are different depending on the season, and there are differences and subdivisions within each season. There are twenty-four microseasons—early summer, late summer, and so on. We are very sensitive to the seasons, and have words in Japanese to identify the different parts of the seasons, such as *Hashiri* [early season], *Shun* [in the middle of the season], *Nagori* [the season is almost ending], and *Ideai* [a period of time when *Hashiri* and *Nagori* are combined]. *Ideai* is a very short, very rarefied period of time, so eating any foods that exist during this time are particularly sought after and special. For example, *hamo* [a fish] is around from July through September. Matsutake mushrooms show up in September and October. For maybe one week in September, they will both be available—this time is very special. Some years, they may not even coincide.

It is important for people to eat according to the seasons; otherwise, foods are not as delicious or as healthy. The human body desires seasonal foods and all five senses are engaged when eating a *kaiseki* meal, from the aromas, textures, sounds, and so on.

What does it take to be a good chef?

A good chef contributes to society, make customers happy. He innovates, he doesn't give up. He is honest. He studies and is motivated. I am still studying.

What is your earliest food memory?

Crab cream croquettes that my mother made. They were very soft. I loved them. After I started cooking, I asked my mom for the recipe, but she lost it and can't cook them anymore!

For you, what does it mean to be Japanese?

People often think that one of the good things about the Japanese is our consideration for others. I think this has been important since the Edo period. For example, when using umbrellas, people are sure not to bump into each other. There is evidence of this in paintings and stories. Japanese care about others, and doing something for someone else's well-being is important. With the cooking here at Kohaku, it's the same concept. We are proud of what we do. Same with the fisherman who wants to catch the best tuna, the artisan who wants to make the best bonito. Everyone's collective spirit is important. This is what it means to be Japanese, to care for community.

If you could meet anyone in public life, who would it be?

Nobunaga Oda, a sixteenth-century *daimyo* [feudal ruler].

Hideyoshi Toyotomi, a samurai, *daimyo*, general, warrior, and politician.

Ieyasu Tokugawa, the founder and first shogun of the Tokugawa shogunate of Japan.

What is your favorite word?

Arigato [thank you].

WAGYU BEEF-WRAPPED SEA URCHIN

This is a summer dish. I wanted to make a cold dish using beef because summer in Japan is very hot and humid. During the summer months, it is important to have meat for protein and energy as people get tired easily.

SHOYU-AN SAUCE

1 cup dashi stock

2 teaspoons mirin

1 tablespoon soy sauce

1 tablespoon sugar

2 teaspoons tapioca starch mixed with 2 teaspoons water

EGGPLANT AND PEPPER

1 quart dashi stock

3 tablespoons mirin

1 tablespoon soy sauce

1 tablespoon sugar

Safflower oil, for frying

4 ounces Japanese eggplant, peeled and halved lengthwise

1 tablespoon seeded and julienned mangan ji (red pepper) or small red bell pepper

BEEF AND UNI

4 ounces Wagyu beef sirloin, sliced thinly against the grain to make 8 slices

24 pieces of *uni* (sea urchin)

4 pinches of chopped chives

4 pinches of kombu salt

4 pinches of ground sesame seeds

SERVES 4

To make the shoyu-an sauce, combine the dashi, mirin, soy sauce, and sugar in a medium saucepan and place over medium heat. Just before it comes to a boil, add the tapioca starch–water mixture slowly, while stirring, until the sauce thickens. Remove from the heat, let cool, and refrigerate until cold.

To make the eggplant, combine the dashi, mirin, soy sauce, and sugar in a medium saucepan. Heat over low heat, stirring, until the sugar is dissolved. Remove from the heat and let cool, transfer to a bowl, cover, and chill until ready to use.

Bring a medium pot of water to a simmer that you will use to blanch the eggplant after frying, then lower the heat and keep hot.

Pour safflower oil into a 6-quart pot until the pot is halfway full and bring to 360°F over high heat. Add the eggplant and deep-fry until it's a nice golden color, about 1 minute. With a spider skimmer or slotted spoon, transfer the eggplant to a paper towel and let sit for a few seconds to drain. Make sure the hot water bath is not at a boil and add the eggplant to the water for about 10 seconds to remove any excess oil. Put the eggplant on fresh paper towels again to remove the water. Finally, transfer the eggplant to the cold dashi stock mixture and marinate for 1 to 5 hours. Then transfer the eggplant to a paper towel again to remove any excess dashi.

In a small saucepan, pour just enough safflower oil to coat the bottom and heat over medium heat. Add the mangan ji and sauté until slightly wilted, about 20 seconds.

To make the beef, bring a medium pot of water to 160°F. Cook the beef shabu-shabu-style, holding one slice at a time with chopsticks and adding it to the hot water without letting go, until it just barely changes color, about 3 seconds. Place on paper towel to dab off the water. Repeat with remaining slices and place in refrigerator for 5 minutes. Put three pieces of uni on each slice of beef and roll tightly.

Cut the eggplant halves in half to make four pieces. Place a piece of eggplant at the top of each dish or bowl, then the two pieces of rolled beef. Place one-fourth of the sautéed mangan ji on top. Pour about 3 tablespoons cold sauce over the top. Sprinkle with a pinch each of chives, kombu salt, and ground sesame seeds. Serve immediately.

NOTE: You can buy ground sesame seeds in Japanese markets or grind them yourself at home.

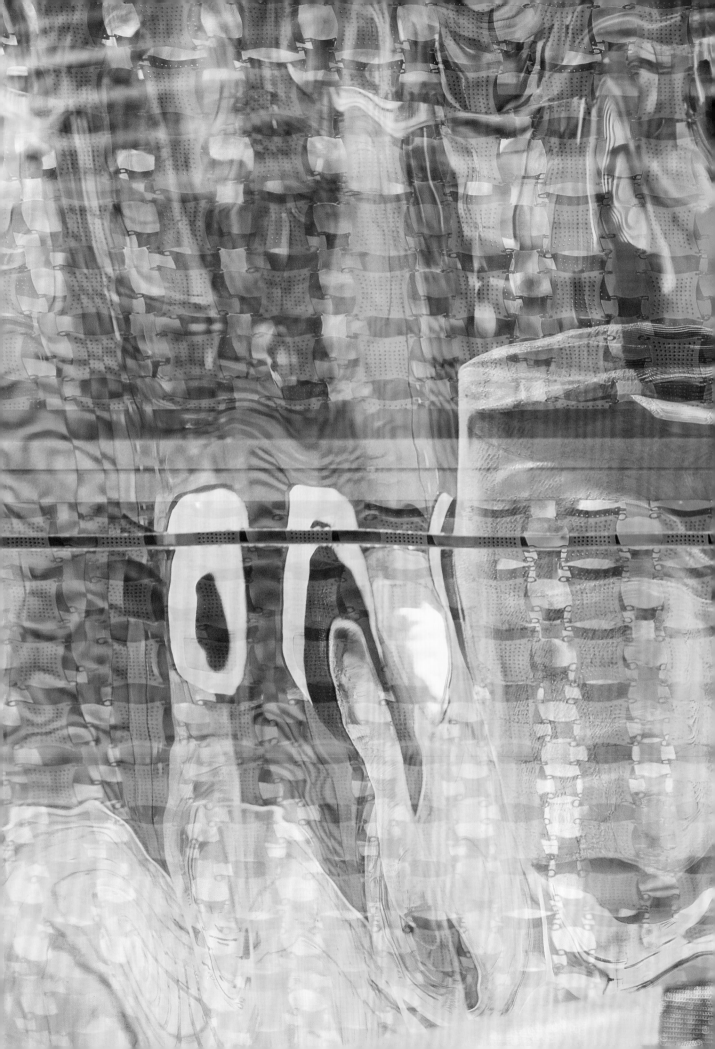

LIONEL
BECCAT

ESQUISSE

ART

EXPRESSION

Lionel Beccat is a culinary artist. His medium happens to be food, but it could easily have been film, painting, fashion, or architecture. His appreciation for art in all its forms sets him apart as a chef. Beccat feels in a heightened manner and sees details that most people don't notice—the tilt of a hat, someone's particular gait, the pattern of water droplets on a window. At his restaurant Esquisse, he paints small abstract watercolors that rest upon the center of each place setting, foreshadowing the sensory meal to come.

When I speak with Beccat, we rarely discuss food or technique. In fact, he prefers not to. Instead we talk extensively, always in French, about architecture, cinema—any of the arts—as a way to understand life and the process of creating. At one afternoon meeting, films are the prism through which we discuss the poignant expression of life's complexities: impossibility depicted in *In The Mood for Love*, and its masterful use of shadow, light, color, and design; or the significance and value of conflict in *Habla Con Ella* (*Talk to Her*). Large life questions that might seem daunting to others are never avoided with Beccat. He does not shy away from dissent, darkness, or sadness, which contributes to the complexity of his dishes. When I eat Beccat's food, I'm struck not only by the delicate beauty before me, but also the intensity and layers of flavors. At Esquisse, I perceive flavors that I do not usually taste.

Beccat, forty, is a soulful man who harbors a constant and potent need for expression; each day is a chance to feed his being and to quench his thirst for living. His meals are sensory voyages; each dish is titled like a piece of art, such as *Retranscrire* (To Transform) and *Force Tellurique* (Earth Force). The flavors in Beccat's dishes are multidimensional, with hidden ingredients that surprise me. Together with his graceful use of texture and color, Beccat's understanding of the depth and potential of dining is clear.

Born in Corsica of a Sicilian mother and Tunisian father, Beccat grew up in Marseille, France. He has made Tokyo his home since 2006, and treasures the profoundly beautiful aspects of life in Japan, especially in the culinary realm.

When I ask a question, Beccat squints a bit, touches his fingers to his close-cropped beard, and pauses in reflection. Daylight accents his smoky hazel eyes, as he delves into a response that is substantial and frank, emblematic of someone who wishes to know and be known. He is the only chef who mulls over our in-person discussions and then voluntarily follows up days later with emails elaborating on what he is trying to express. He even includes quotes from artists who he esteems, like the distinguished Mexican architect Luis Barragán.

"Anyone who has never known the feeling of solitude, the feeling of abandonment and of idleness, cannot respond to my architecture" is one such quote I received. Perhaps in some way the same can be said of Beccat's work. Those who embrace the complexity and depth of life, seeking to artfully reconcile and express its many contradictions, complexities, and essence, will revel in Beccat's edible creations.

INTERVIEW

Why did you move to Japan?

I came to Tokyo in 2006 to open the Michel Troisgros restaurant as sous chef, then executive chef. I was at Michel Troisgros until 2012, when I was given the opportunity to open my own restaurant.

Why do you cook?

Because I need to express myself.

I studied history in university to become a professor. When I realized that I didn't want to become a professor, I chose cooking. I wasn't entirely sure, though I had a feeling that I would love to cook. I needed more exultation, something to fill me up and nourish me. I wanted to be pollinated, so to speak.

Cooking was always about Mom and home, about affection. Food is proof of love, it's intimate, and stronger than saying I love you. I thought that it might be fantastic to cook all the time and make this my career, my discipline. You think that you make the food, but it's the food that is making you. Making food changes you, feeds you, affects you, improves you, nourishes you. Cooking is an act of freedom.

When my dishes arrive on the table, I no longer exist. Once they come out from the kitchen, my vision is finished. It belongs to you now; it is your dish. It is now your emotions, your flavors. Cooking is like cinema and music, it's like what is made by those who listen, those who look. The energy I put into my dishes is from my inspiration and my thoughts. I give you all the space you need to interpret the dish I have made. If it makes you travel, if you adore it or not—it doesn't belong to me anymore.

Where do you find your happiness and meaning?

In cooking, I find grace and happiness and things make sense. Synchronicity . . . I am using all my senses and everything comes together. I use my poetry, my spirit, everything that makes me human to cook, everything I am in my life, all aspects of myself.

What is your earliest food memory?

Every Sunday evening, my mother would make pizza from the week's bread. She would use the leftovers of many things to make a pizza and salad. It is the strongest memory because there's simplicity, there's repetition—my mother's care, the family dynamic. This shows what cooking really is. This is why I love what I do, why I cook—it's everything around the act of making the actual food.

How do you think living in Japan informs your style?

Cooking is a human language. It is perhaps the first language we all learn. We can understand by eating—it is universal. I am an *enfant du monde* [child of the world], so I don't feel obligated to respond to my French identity in my cooking. I grew up with more Italian and Arab cooking than with French cooking.

Here in Japan, you realize the immensity of Japanese cuisine. You learn so much here and need time to digest all this information. You are obligated to take all that you have learned here and translate and inscribe everything. It is one of the most beautiful and most complex culinary traditions. It's a font of inspiration that is extraordinary and unique.

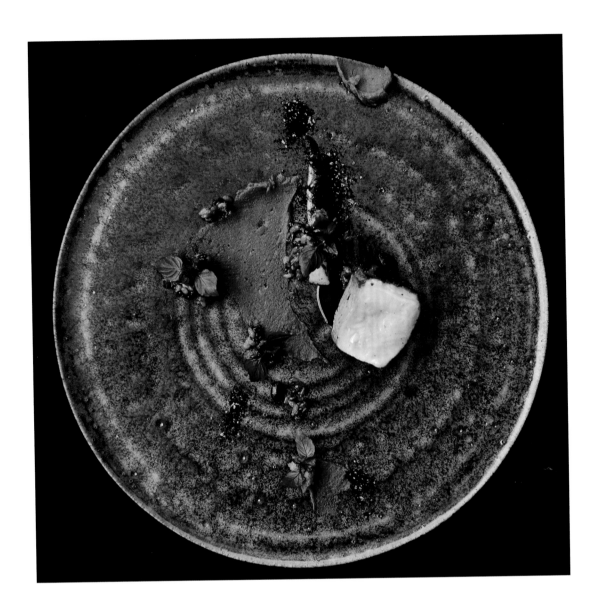

For you, what does it mean to be Japanese?

The Japanese are children of a hostile island. They are insular, with a culture that stretches back thousands of years. They spend their lives glorifying and interpreting all of the codes and rules from living on this island. It's a difficult island naturewise, with a lot of natural disasters. Living and creating a society here was very difficult. To survive, the Japanese had to invent many ways to adapt. Nature shaped their spirit and way of being. The Japanese established one of the most beautiful civilizations on Earth.

As a foreigner, what is life like here?

I have the feeling that I am living an imaginary life. I feel like I'm living a life I never should have had. Nothing predestined me to come here. I am from the Mediterranean, from Marseille, which has nothing to do with Japan. But I have totally taken off.

Living here has made it possible to understand myself more. I stick out. I like this. I obey rules and a code that is counter to my nature. And this is interesting. I don't belong to France and I don't belong to Japan, either. I no longer have daily stimuli that reinforce my roots. I am free.

What are some of the most valuable things you have learned from living in Japan—as a person and a chef?

A sense of the essential. Not minimalism, but purity.

My definition of beauty changed here. My eyes changed. My tastes changed. It has been redefined here to what I consider beautiful. No one wears perfume here. To wear perfume means to announce your presence, and that's the opposite of the Japanese spirit. For the Japanese, beauty should be hidden, you should discover it slowly. Nothing should be revealed all at once.

I discovered Japanese artists here. They are actually the freest in the world—they are crazy. They live in a difficult society. It is oppressive. And to be able to express yourself to counter this oppression—they are amazingly creative. This has all changed me, it has calmed me. Silence is an art form here.

What do you like most about Tokyo and what do you think makes it different from other cities around the world?

It's the first city where I feel a distinct spirit. It's like a female entity. Tokyo is female—calm and furious at the same time. She inherited millions of treasures, but she is still pragmatic. She is ambiguous. I am affected by her fury; one must live by her rhythms. She is always moving, sometimes exhausting; she reinvents herself all the time. She presents many challenges, yet I feel as if anything is possible. Things get done here.

Tell me about your relationship with art, and the significance of the name Esquisse.

Art is nourishment. It's indirect but it is always there. It infuses me and everything I do, and then unconsciously art works its way into my food.

The creative process is what interests me and inspires me as much as the actual work. It's the methodology of the artist.

The search for oneself through the creative process. I don't ask myself anymore about the finality of my work and how I arrive at the results. This is why I called my restaurant Esquisse [sketch in French]. It symbolizes all the ways and paths an artist takes to realize something—all the failures and false starts. I am as interested in what has inspired and pushed an artist to create something as I am with the actual result of that effort.

Cooking is the only discipline that requires all five senses. It is like being in a trance—sight, taste, sound, feel, smell. Tell me about another art that is like this. It is the most complete.

Tell me about the thought behind the little watercolor designs placed on the plates at Esquisse.

To give diners a little sketch conveys more than a menu. I like to use kanji and to paint and include all that inspired me to make the menu. I like to show what illuminated me to cook what I am cooking. Some people understand the design at the end of the meal more than at the beginning.

If you couldn't be a chef anymore, what would you do instead?

I would be a carpenter or a hermit.

If you could share a meal with anyone, who would it be?

Socrates, because I'd like to ask him how he was able to create a philosophy that proves itself to be more and more true.

Éric Contona, because he is a true tortured genius.

Jacques Prévert, the poet, so he can read me his poetry.

Andy Warhol, so that he can talk to me about Basquiat.

Jackson Pollock, so that he can explain how his unique way of painting came to him.

What is your favorite word?

Ephemeral.

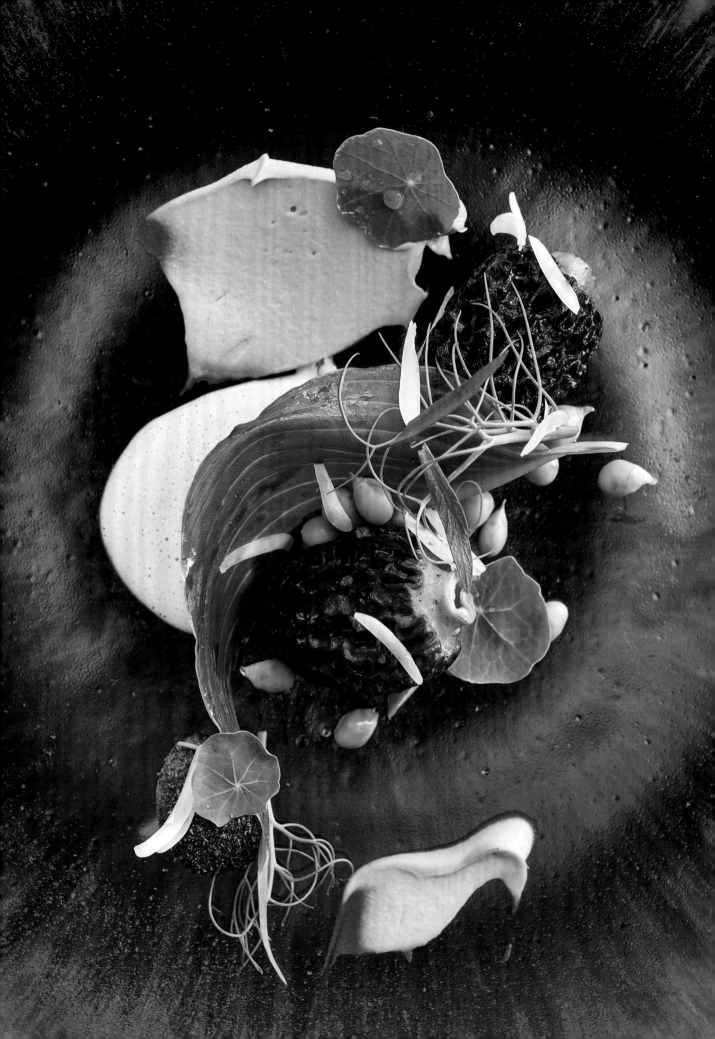

"SPRING TREASURE" MOREL MUSHROOMS WITH QUAIL EGGS AND ALMOND

I composed this dish with the image of a wild field during a morning in spring, when the sun reveals the night's humidity. The morning dew appears as if some sort of mysterious regeneration happened overnight. At this moment, the scent of the humidity of a spring field is evident in the morels.

QUAIL EGGS

4 quail eggs

2 tablespoons white wine

1 teaspoon mashed black garlic

½ teaspoon sugar

MUSHROOMS

2 tablespoons extra-virgin olive oil

1 teaspoon unsalted butter

12 large morel mushrooms, trimmed

2 tablespoons white wine

BROCCOLI PUREE

4 ounces broccoli florets

4 teaspoons olive oil

¾ teaspoon almond paste

SAUCE

¾ cup plus 1 tablespoon white wine

¼ cup chopped shallot

¼ cup chopped carrot

1 teaspoon chopped fresh tarragon

6 tablespoons heavy cream

4 teaspoons unsalted butter

ALMOND MIXTURE

2 raw almonds, finely slivered

¼ teaspoon almond oil

½ teaspoon orange juice

12 broccoli leaves, minced

6 urui or spinach leaves

10 fresh peas or edible radish seeds

3 pea shoot tendrils or broccoli sprouts, finely chopped, for garnish

Fresh tarragon and nasturtium leaves, for garnish

SERVES 2

To make the quail eggs, prepare an ice bath. Bring a pot of water to 150°F over medium heat, then add the quail eggs and cook for 7 minutes, until medium boiled. Transfer the quail eggs to the ice bath to cool. Combine the white wine, black garlic, and sugar in a bowl. Peel the eggs and place in the white wine mixture, turn to coat, and refrigerate for 24 hours.

To make the mushrooms, the next day, warm the olive oil and butter in a frying pan over medium heat. Add the morels and cook for about 3 minutes, until softened. Add the white wine and deglaze the pan for 30 seconds, until the wine has evaporated. Remove from the heat and set aside.

To make the broccoli puree, bring a pot of salted water to a boil over high heat. Add the broccoli and cook for 4 minutes, until tender when pierced with a knife. Drain. While the broccoli is still hot, place in a blender or food processor with the olive oil and almond paste and blend into a puree. Set aside and keep warm.

To make the sauce, combine the white wine, shallot, carrot, and tarragon in a saucepan and cook over medium heat until the mixture is reduced by half, about 10 minutes. Strain out the solids, add the cream and butter, and continue to cook until the butter melts. Keep warm.

To make the almond mixture, combine all of the ingredients and set aside at room temperature.

Place a few spoonfuls of the broccoli puree and sauce on each plate. Coat the quail eggs with the minced broccoli leaves, place one quail egg on top of the sauce, and cover with a few urui leaves. Arrange the mushrooms around the egg. Place the other egg off to the side. Sprinkle with the peas, almond mixture, pea tendrils, tarragon, and nasturtium leaves. Serve right away.

NOTE: You need to start the quail eggs one day ahead. Black or fermented garlic can be found at specialty spice shops and some grocery stores.

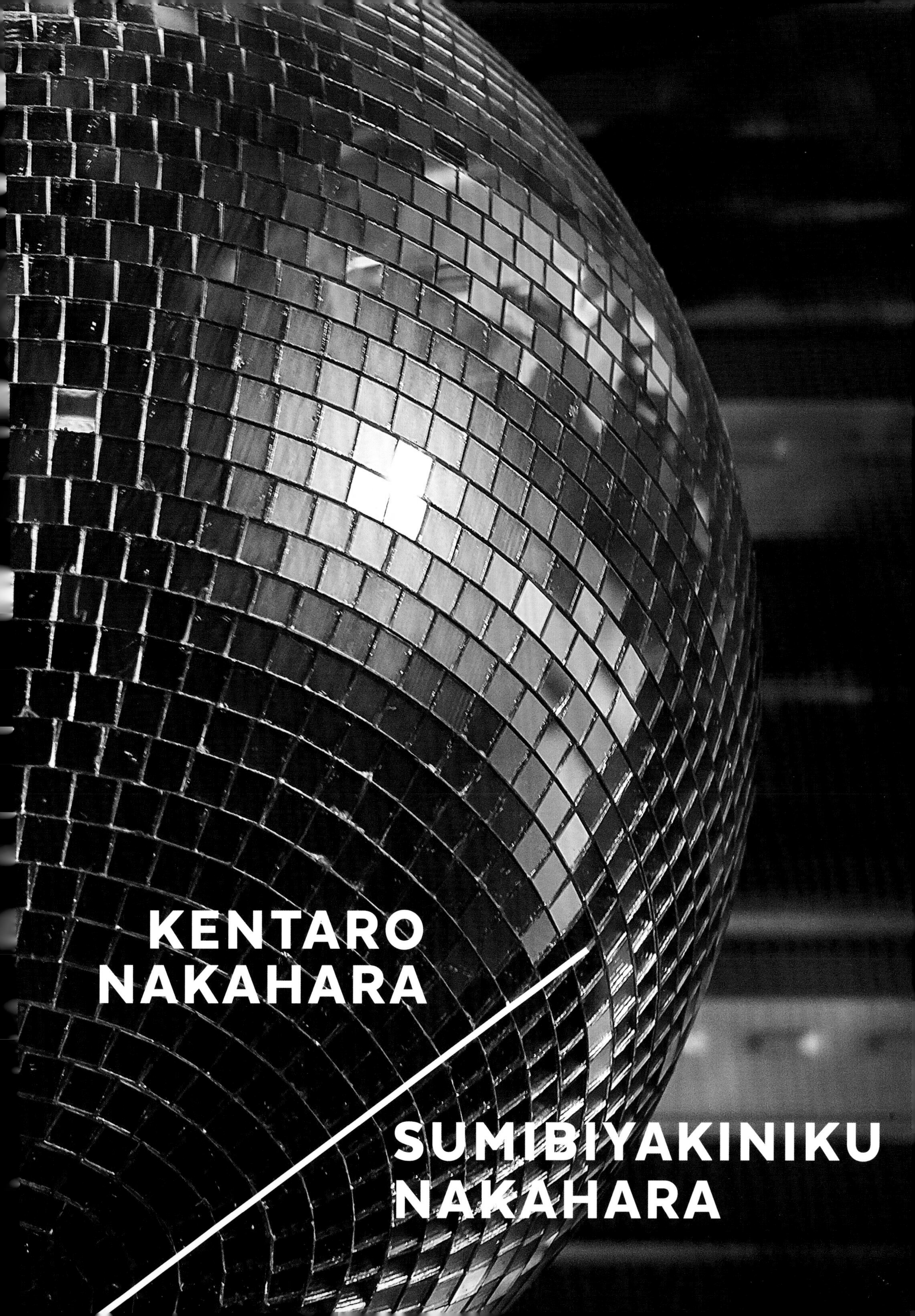

KENTARO
NAKAHARA

SUMIBIYAKINIKU
NAKAHARA

CARE

SINCERITY

More than anyone I have come to know here in Japan, Kentaro Nakahara adores sushi. On occasion, it even moves him to tears. Nakahara marvels at the grace and beauty of his favorite sushi master's technique as if he were sitting in a box at a Kabuki performance. Sometimes he gasps, covering his eyes in a dramatic moment of disbelief. His reverence for excellent sushi has no bounds. Yet Nakahara is not a sushi chef himself. He is a *yakiniku* (grilled beef) master, one of the most outstanding in Tokyo. He applies the philosophy, artfulness, and precision of the finest sushi techniques to the preparation of the finest beef at his restaurant, Sumibiyakiniku Nakahara.

Nakahara, born in San Jose, California, is a son, father, husband, and DJ, who became a chef later than most other Tokyo chefs. "I was very poor. I became a chef out of necessity, not because I had always dreamed of it," he told me, with a disarming degree of candor. Authenticity makes Nakahara so likable; he does not pretend to be anyone other than who he is. He is also generous and caring; when I arrived in Tokyo, he persistently asked how I was settling in, and helped in any way he could. He models his life on the credo, "We are all a chain," meaning that we are all interconnected.

The artisanal Tajima beef personally selected at auction and used in his barbecue is Nakahara's specialty. As he ties his trademark blue-and-white scarf tightly around his head, he explains that this beef is known for its highly desirable *shimofuri* (the marbling of fat through the meat). He takes a cut of sirloin out of a refrigerator, unwrapping a piece of white silk fabric that helps the beef retain its color, moisture, and velvety texture.

Nakahara's clientele is obsessed with his beef *omakase* (chef's choice) menu, which includes an astonishing array of cuts for *yakiniku*, plus beef *nigiri*, *bibimbap*, and the imitable off-menu beef *sando* (sandwich). Silver and vibrant red chairs, luminous blue tile, and black touches make up the palette of the open, contemporary, and smokeless loft space that is Sumibiyakiniku Nakahara. An oversized silver outline of a Picassso-inspired bull emblazons one wall. As he prepares *gyu katsu* (beef *katsu*), the perfume of the sizzling rice oil wafts in the air. The texture of the beef is moist, soft, and, yes, buttery; and the outside is crisp and golden with just the right amount of sea salt. Nakahara stands behind the counter grinning from ear to ear, his pride, sincerity, and love for what he does as special as his *yakiniku*.

INTER VIEW

Did you grow up in Tokyo?

I was born in San Jose, California, and I lived there for four years. Then I went back and forth, living here and in the United States, until we moved back here to Tokyo when I was nine years old.

What gives you your sense of purpose?

Hmm, this is difficult, because I rarely think that way. Maybe I ask myself, "Am I doing things the right way?"

I am actually self-trained. About thirteen years ago, I went to Tokyo Central Meat Market in Shibaura and said I wanted to buy meat, the same way as chefs directly buy fish at the Tsukiji fish market, but I was always turned down. For a week, I went every day at 7 a.m. and each time I was turned away. Then one day when I arrived they prepared white rubber boots and a white coat to dress me like a butcher, and they finally said that I could enter. I asked some of the vendors to teach me how to butcher. The best beef in Shibaura is just as good as the fish is at Tsukiji.

When well-known chefs come to eat at my restaurant, I feel inspired and as if I must be doing things correctly. Chefs like Hideki Ishikawa, Takashi Saito, Zaiyu Hasegawa (page 3), and Keiji Nakazawa. I like focusing on one thing, like beef. I even have a special license for serving raw beef, a unique privilege claimed by few chefs in Japan.

Why didn't you become a sushi chef?

I never dreamed of becoming a chef like I am now. But after doing this job for some time, I have had many opportunities to connect and become friends with many sushi *shokunin* [master artisans]. And I started realizing just how much I really love sushi. It is too late now to train myself to become a sushi chef, but I still respect them so deeply.

What is your earliest food memory?

Eating sushi in San Jose.

For you, what does it mean to be Japanese, and how does this affect your life as a chef?

The way I act. When I am somewhere else, I feel that I'm something different. Abroad, I feel like people are more focused on themselves. In Japan, we are always so worried about others and are always following the rules. We have a common sense of shared values. We all have a similar mind-set in Japan. Japanese are more stressed—we don't laugh as much. We don't want to appear arrogant. We don't talk too much, just show. This is also how I cook and run my restaurant.

My parents lived for many years in California, my dad for thirty years. I also went to a Christian school in Aoyama, and many of my earliest friends were Japanese but felt American because they had lived in America, like I had. Because of these things, I picked up some American attitudes. I realized that I wanted to be more direct, honest, and true to myself rather than follow the crowd, which is more typically Japanese.

What is your favorite word?

Seicho, which means growth.

What is one of your favorite films and why?

The Godfather. I like it because of the family story and the rules they followed: never go against the family. It's the ultimate story of humanity.

BEEF CUTLET (GYUKATSU)

The original meat for katsuretsu *or* katsu *was beef rather than pork. Deep-frying was introduced to Japan from Europe back in the Meiji period, so this is inherently a Western, or* yōshoku, *dish. The crispy coating keeps the juiciness of the beef sealed in; the inside is buttery. It's a simple dish but the quality of the beef is incredibly important. I find that rice bran oil is the best for frying. You can present it simply with finely shredded cabbage or in a sandwich (*katsu sando*) between slices of white bread.*

Rice bran oil, for deep-frying

1 piece round cut of Wagyu beef tenderloin, sliced ½ inch thick, at room temperature

½ cup flour

2 eggs, lightly beaten

½ cup panko bread crumbs

Salt and freshly ground pepper

½ cup finely shredded cabbage

SERVES 1

Fill a 6-quart pan with about 2 inches of rice bran oil and heat over medium heat until it reaches 325°F.

Dab the beef with a paper towel to remove any excess moisture.

Put the flour in a shallow bowl, the eggs in a second bowl, and the bread crumbs in a third bowl. Season both sides of the beef with salt and pepper. Dredge the beef in the flour, shaking off the excess. Dip in the egg, then dredge in the bread crumbs.

Deep-fry the beef cutlet for about 4 minutes, until golden brown. Use chopsticks to transfer to paper towels and let rest for 2 to 3 minutes.

Cut the cutlet in half and place on a serving plate with the cabbage. Serve right away.

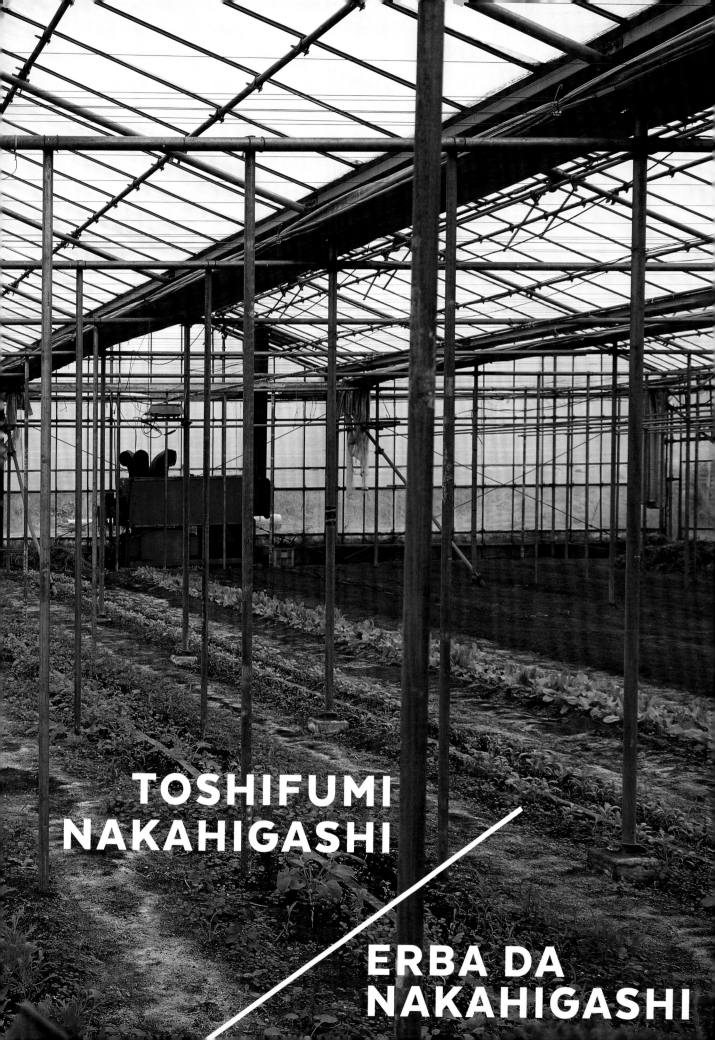

TOSHIFUMI
NAKAHIGASHI

ERBA DA
NAKAHIGASHI

ELEGANCE

HEART

Toshifumi Nakahigashi expresses an unhindered joy and love for Italy, declaring that his heart might be in Kyoto, the city of his birth, but his soul is most definitely in Italy. He went to live there at eighteen, first to learn the language and then to find a job. He traveled the country, dining at a range of restaurants to learn about and understand Italian cuisine. He established a deeply rewarding and fascinating life in Italy, working at many top Michelin-starred restaurants, including Arnolfo Ristorante outside Siena. Nakahigashi has a deep understanding of Italian technique, and his refined and elevated tastes and perspective make for an enchanting dining experience at Erba da Nakahigashi.

An elegant jewel of a restaurant, Erba da Nakahigashi is fresh, smart, refined, and thoroughly stylish with tones of dark gray and black and a series of cascading lights hovering over the counter. Thirty-five-year-old Nakahigashi hails from generations of lauded chefs; his grandmother was a pioneering chef who specialized in mountain vegetables, and his father is the famous two-star Michelin chef Sojiki Nakahigashi, a master of *kaiseki* cuisine (haute cuisine).

Speaking with Nakahigashi in Italian and spending time with him is a joyful experience because he is so joyful himself. He smiles often and intersperses his spoken Italian with colloquialisms; he learned the language well and speaks with fondness of the friends he made in Italy. Recalling his first mentor, chef Gaetano Trovato of Arnolfo Ristorante, his great affection and regard is palpable. Nakahigashi also mentions a year working at Plaza Athenée in Paris as a supremely instructive experience, yet not as transformative or viscerally nourishing as his time in Italy.

As he reminisces about the food, friends, farmers, and architecture he left behind in Tuscany, Nakahigashi wistfully acknowledges that he dreams of Italy and misses it daily. He is also attached to Japan, however, and finds that the two countries are culinarily strikingly similar. Nakahigashi touches upon his deep-rooted respect for ingredients and terroir as we drive to meet the farmer who provides the roses for his squab dish. One of his mantras—*using few ingredients and preparing them in a complex fashion equals respect for the ingredients*—is a philosophy he sees as foundational to Italian and Japanese food.

The comparable umami that is present in both cuisines makes an Italian restaurant in Japan the most natural of phenomena, he says. As I savor a spoonful of umami-rich gorgonzola mousse, I nod in agreement and make a reservation to return.

INTERVIEW

What made you decide to become an Italian chef?

When I was thirteen, I ate *spaghetti al pomodoro* near my house in Kyoto at a restaurant called Casa Bianca. It amazed me. It was so tasty, but simple with minimal ingredients. The perfume of the olive oil, the way it was cooked, was perfect, as was the Parmigiano-Reggiano. From that moment, I wanted to learn everything about Italy. I liked and appreciated Kyoto cuisine but thought it was very complicated. I somehow thought Italian food would be easier to make well, but it is not.

I always knew I would open a restaurant in Japan, and I knew I had to plan how to do this. I wanted to learn about traditional Italian cuisine before Michelin-starred food. I wanted to start in Tuscany, where there is a lot of respect for ingredients. The first dish I had when I arrived was rabbit liver with shallots. The second was *pici* [thick hand-rolled pasta, similar to spaghetti] with pork ragù. I understood that this traditional food was being prepared in a very modern and elegant way. It touched my soul. I loved it!

Tell me your thoughts about cooking.

Cooking is interesting to me—how all the ingredients change according to each cuisine. In Italian cuisine, if the ingredient is great, the dish can be great as that is the essence. I come from a family of chefs. When a chef like me brings more complicated technique and inspiration from my own personal life, a dish becomes more interesting. From the age of eighteen, I have had a lot of the spirit of Italy in me. I think Italian food is about tasting the essence of the ingredient. I put my life into it.

The workmanship can certainly be complicated, but the result on the plate must not, because if the flavors are too complicated, one does not taste all the ingredients or respect them. The fragrance of an ingredient, for example, should be distinguishable. Too many ingredients mixed together and the chef runs the risk of making it too hard to perceive or distinguish them, and the dish fails. For example, I would never pair uni with beef, but here in Japan, they do it.

Tell me a bit about what you thought of Italy.

It was easy to be with so many nice Italian people. Friends would invite me to their homes, where I would taste their mother's food. Even the architecture was very interesting. Some friends' families had country homes with farms and animals, like rabbits. I worked at all Michelin-starred restaurants, where there were staff from all over Italy and even from Japan. I didn't miss Japan too much.

Do you think there are commonalities between Japanese and Italian cuisine?

Yes. Dashi and *spaghetti al pomodoro* have the same umami. It's the glutamic acid, one of the elements of umami, in the tomato sauce, like kombu in Japanese food. There is also glutamic acid in Japanese dashi and in Parmigiano-Reggiano. All of these are similar. And the idea of simplicity and deep respect for ingredients is in both cultures. I think bread, extra-virgin olive oil, and sea salt in Italy is like rice and *tsukemono* [preserved vegetables] here.

For you, what does it mean to be Japanese?

It means to be malleable. Aspects of our culture came from China, Korea, Thailand, and other countries. Many cultural elements arrive here, even from the United States. We are always trying to improve our culture and our cooking. We like to adapt and change things, even improve them sometimes. Yes, past generations used to be much more rigid. For example, five hundred years ago, there was no frying in Japan, until it came via Portugal. If we didn't learn how to fry from the Portuguese, we wouldn't have tempura.

Is eating *spaghetti al pomodoro* your earliest first food memory?

No, when I was four or five years old, I remember eating *tochi mochi* [sweet rice cake] made of a chestnutlike nut found in the mountains outside Kyoto. The cook at my grandparent's restaurant handed it to me—it was nice and fresh and soft. I loved it.

What fuels your creativity in the kitchen?

I take inspiration from the garden of the mountains—any mountains really. I love the air and all the seasons. The seasons were important in Tuscany, too. We went often to the vineyards, and in Lago di Garda, I went to the mountains and we picked wild herbs. There was also a garden behind the restaurant. I also take inspiration from Picasso and the ceramicist Kitaoji Rosanjin, and the painter Jakuchu, who painted three hundred years ago.

What is your favorite word?

I have a phrase that I like:

Jinseide okorukotoha subete sarano uede okoru.

"If it happens in life, it happens on the plate."

What is one of your favorite films?

I will give you two: *Big Night* and *Cinema Paradiso*. *Big Night* is about two brothers who wanted to defend the traditions of Italian food, I like that. I like *Cinema Paradiso* for how it shows the passage of time, the history of Italy, and how things change.

PUMPKIN LASAGNE

The remembrance of the beginning of autumn is evoked with the sweetness of the humble pumpkin and the perfume of the elegant Gorgonzola.

PUMPKIN PUREE

1 small pumpkin (7 ounces), cut in half and seeded

1 clove garlic, peeled

1 rosemary sprig

¾ cup heavy cream

7 tablespoons unsalted butter

PASTA

1 cup plus 2 tablespoons Italian 00 flour, such as Antimo Caputo brand

2 eggs

GORGONZOLA MOUSSE

2 ounces Gorgonzola piccante (or aged Gorgonzola)

1½ tablespoons heavy cream

Butter, for greasing the pan

4 tablespoons grated Parmigiano-Reggiano

Hulled pumpkin seeds, for garnish

SERVES 6 TO 12

Preheat the oven to 325°F.

To make the pumpkin puree, place the pumpkin, garlic, and rosemary on a large sheet of aluminum foil. Wrap the foil tightly to seal and place on a baking sheet. Bake for about 1 hour, until the pumpkin is soft and a toothpick inserted in the center comes out clean. Unwrap and let cool to room temperature, then remove the flesh with a spoon and discard the skin, rosemary, and garlic.

Press the pumpkin through a medium-mesh sieve or chinois into a large bowl.

Place the cream and butter in a saucepan over low heat, stirring occasionally, until the butter has melted. Pour into the pumpkin puree and stir until combined.

To make the pasta, combine the flour and eggs in another bowl, mixing together with your hands and then kneading until a smooth dough forms, about 5 minutes. Gather into a ball and let the dough rest for about 20 minutes.

To make the Gorgonzola mousse, combine the Gorgonzola and heavy cream in a small sauce pan and cook over medium-low heat for about 5 minutes, stirring, until creamy. Pour the mousse into a container and refrigerate for 10 minutes, until thickened. Keep chilled until serving.

Divide the dough into four sections and form each into a rectangle about ½ inch thick. Using a pasta machine, roll out one piece of dough, starting at the largest setting and working your way down until it is 1⁄16 inch thick, or about the second smallest setting. Cut the dough into an 8 by 14-inch sheet. Cover with a kitchen towel and repeat with the remaining dough.

Prepare an ice bath. Bring a large pot of salted water to a boil. Add two pasta sheets and cook for about 1 minute, then drain and put in the ice bath for a few seconds to cool. Remove the pasta sheets from the ice bath with a spider skimmer and spread out on a work surface until dry, or place in the refrigerator covered in towels until ready to assemble. Repeat with the remaining pasta.

Preheat the oven to 400°F. Lightly grease a baking sheet with butter.

Place a pasta sheet on a clean work surface. With a tablespoon, spread some of the pumpkin puree over a pasta sheet in a thin layer. With the long side facing you, roll the pasta into a log shape. Cut it into thirds. Repeat with the remaining three sheets of pasta.

Place the rolled lasagne pieces in the prepared baking sheet and bake for about 10 minutes until lightly browned.

Place one or two lasagne rolls in the center of the serving plates and sprinkle with the Parmigiano-Reggiano. With two spoons, shape the mousse into two quenelles, or oval spoonfuls, and place on top of the lasagna rolls. Sprinkle with the pumpkin seeds and serve right away.

SHUZO
KISHIDA

QUINTESSENCE

SENSITIVITY

RESTRAINT

It is not possible to discuss this generation of Tokyo chefs without including Shuzo Kishida. Chef at Quintessence since 2006, and sole owner since 2011, his restaurant has long been lauded and lavished with awards galore. When the *Michelin Guide* launched in Tokyo in 2007, a year after Quintessence opened, Kishida received three stars at the age of thirty-three, the only Japanese chef of French cuisine awarded this honor. He has kept these stars ever since. He is well known and widely respected for his achievements and culinary gifts, and a reservation at his restaurant is one of the toughest in the world to secure.

All of the chefs in this book revere Kishida for his accomplishments. He has a reputation for being not only painstakingly exacting but also shy and rarely deviating from his daily routine. I was cautioned that he might not allow me to photograph him, which made me all the more interested.

When Kishida emerges from the kitchen, he is formal and reserved, but also gracious and visibly happy to interact in French. He looks younger than his forty-three years. Slight and enveloped in classic whites, there is a wispiness and gentle vulnerability to him.

He agrees to be a part of my project, but stipulates that I will not be allowed in his kitchen—a first in my career. Even Marco Pierre White, not exactly known for permissiveness, allowed me to take photos in his kitchen. I am at first taken aback by this stipulation, but then appreciate this insight into Kishida's way of thinking. He has an aversion to chance and unpredictability. An exceeding level of control is required to maintain his high standards and the status of his restaurant.

The best part of my time with Kishida is the interview. Sitting across the table from me, tranquil, with his hands gently crossed, he is much more candid than I anticipated. He attributes his life as a chef to his parents, who took him to a French restaurant when he was in junior high school. This dinner launched his profound and fervent discovery of self, France, and French food, "all that was bright and beautiful," he says.

Ultimately, Kishida is not shy. He is someone with an extremely rich and vibrant interior life, a veritable aesthete who is highly affected by the world around him. In some ways, it might be true that he has cordoned himself off, removed from the fray. But it is here that he functions best. He has a deep-seated drive for perfection, and is absolutely firm in how to protect all that he has created.

INTERVIEW

Why do you cook?

One of the reasons is my parents. They loved cooking and they took me to restaurants when I was young. My parents both worked. My mother arrived home late at night, so there was no time to cook. She would ask the children, three of us, to cook together to help her. I was the youngest. It was a pleasure for me to help my mother. I made Japanese home cooking. My mother was so pleased, and I felt happy because she thanked me as well. It made me feel good; it was unusual for someone to thank me.

How was your first trip to Paris?

When I arrived, I was twenty-six. I felt touched and moved by Paris. I felt much more free in Paris than in Japan. I worked such long hours in Paris, but I could do everything I wanted. I had to work hard, too, but compared with my experiences in Japan, it wasn't as hard. Sometimes in Tokyo, I was punched and treated badly. Learning in Japan was the strictest in the world at the time.

Tell me about the experience of being awarded three Michelin stars.

I was thirty-three years old. I felt pressure when I received the stars initially, but now I don't feel as pressured. I care more that the customer is pleased and happy. If my mind, my spirit, and principles don't change, I don't think my stars will change. I feel that I am a *shokunin* [master artisan]. Now there are so many celebrity chefs who are not cooking in their restaurants very often. I wouldn't want to be like that. I want to cook and be here all the time. There is nothing else in the world I would rather do than be a chef.

What is your earliest food memory?

My mother would always take a dish and try cooking it in different ways. For example, she made curry with grated ginger or cocoa, or added something new. She was always challenging herself to do something different or better. She liked to innovate.

How did you decide on the design of your restaurant?

No flowers, no pictures, no music. Nothing. I want people focused on the meal. Very simple. Same as my dishes. The only deviation is the entrance.

How do you think growing up in Japan informs your style?

Who I am is always related to my cuisine; it is hard to separate the two. I am my cuisine. In French cuisine, compared to Japanese cuisine, it is very complicated to make one dish. Japanese food is simple but also difficult because umami must be extracted from the ingredients. They are essentially two totally different cuisines, but I make a unique French cuisine with Japanese methods.

If you could share a meal with anyone, who would it be?

My parents. How many more times will I be able to have a meal with my parents? I want to treasure my time with them.

TAKAAKI
SUGITA

/ SUGITA

CHARACTER

HONOR

It is true that sushi chefs tend to glow; they have a superclean, buffed sheen to them, including their oft-shaved heads. Takaaki Sugita most certainly glows. He looks as if he emerged not long ago from a detoxifying sauna. His close-cropped hair is visibly coarse and prickly, and he is dressed in all white, down to his *tabi* (split-toe) socks. Historically, strict cleanliness has always been of utmost importance within the discipline of sushi. One of the tenets of a proper sushi chef is *isagiyosa*, which means to be brave, pure, clean, and manly.

I visit Sugita at his eponymous restaurant, located in a subterranean space. It is traditional but feels brand-new, dominated by a Hinoki cypress counter. Ten chairs are covered in cream-colored cotton upholstery, and eclectic handmade pottery is displayed. In just a few minutes, I hear the scurrying of wooden *geta* (traditional footwear). It is Sugita.

As Sugita greets me, he smiles and bows; his voice is both powerful and warm. There is a sweetness in his eyes and the tilt of his eyebrows; he radiates kindness, wholesomeness even. He exudes an air of grace and correctness, all of which makes Sugita, at forty-three, a much loved and admired talent within Tokyo's highly discerning gastronomic corridors. He is implicitly trusted as the steward of a cuisine that is closely linked to the essence and history of Japan—a cuisine that holds purity, simplicity, and minimalism in high esteem; a cuisine where nothing is hidden.

Tokyo chefs often tell me that sushi is the food they prefer on their days off. It runs deep in the country's collective consciousness. Sugita is where many of the city's finest chefs come to eat magnificent sushi—it is booked nearly a year in advance. It is not in the guidebooks, and Sugita himself is not all over social media. Not one for self-promotion, he functions below the fray, unconcerned with accolades, and would prefer to stay in Japan rather than travel abroad. Highly respected as both a sushi master and individual, for his skills and his character, Sugita is guided by *bushido* (the way of the warrior), which stresses self-discipline and honor. This may explain Sugita's centered and solid energy.

Eating at Sugita is about more than enjoying exceptional sushi. It is a transcendent experience as powerful as music or fine art, exceedingly moving and otherworldly. It is about the discovery of the soul of a country.

INTERVIEW

Did you grow up in Tokyo?

I am from Chiba and was there until I was eighteen. After high school, I came to Tokyo. I knew I wanted to be a sushi chef, so I knew I had to come to Tokyo, the most important city for sushi.

Why a sushi chef?

When I was in junior high school, I saw a TV drama based on the life a young sushi trainee becoming a sushi chef, *Iki no ii-yatsu*. It seemed both beautiful and cool to me—how the sushi is made, the movement. And also the appearance of sushi chefs appealed to me.

When I was in high school, a friend of mine worked in a sushi restaurant. He asked if I could replace him part-time. When I worked in the back preparing tea, there was a little boy who came and the sushi chef served him. The little boy smiled so broadly, and this made me feel great, to see that people could have this reaction. I knew then this would be my job.

Tell me about the significance of sushi in Japanese culture.

With sushi, the chef uses his own hands to serve people directly. We don't hide anything behind the counter. Communication is important, not just the cooking. Sushi is such a big part of Japanese identity, especially for Japanese chefs.

Sushi is very simple—rice, fish, soy sauce, vinegar. We have been eating this for so many years. Sushi cuts out anything that is not necessary. In and of itself, it is pure and brave.

Reisetsu [propriety] and the relationship between the master and apprentice are important; so, too, with the master and customer. There are rules for a sushi chef—every sushi chef prays to gods, greets everyone in a certain way. *Bushido* [the way of the samurai] is also a part of sushi cuisine.

What is your earliest food memory?

My mother cooked; she was not a great cook, but I liked her food. My father used to go the mountains to collect the Japanese yam called *jinenjo*—it's big and long. They are hard to find. My dad would grate it to make *tororo* [a sticky form of the yam], and I thought it was tasty but also itchy around my mouth.

If you could meet anyone in public life, who would it be?

Ieyasu Tokugawa, a shogun in the Edo period. He wasn't so talented, but he was very patient and learned a lot. He was known for making an effort. At the time, there was a lot of fighting, and he worked for peace. He must have had a very strong spirit. I admire this.

Is this what it means to you to be Japanese?

Not only strong spirit, but patience, the ability to learn. A sense of honor. Not to be too snobbish. To be centered. Even if you want to celebrate in front of someone who lost, you just don't show your exuberance in front of the loser, for example. You don't taunt them and brag. If you are centered, you can be kind to others. This way, you can be stable no matter what.

What is your favorite word?

I have a phrase that I like:

Keikoutonarumo gyugotonarunakare.

"It is better to be a big fish in a small pond rather than a small fish in a big pond."

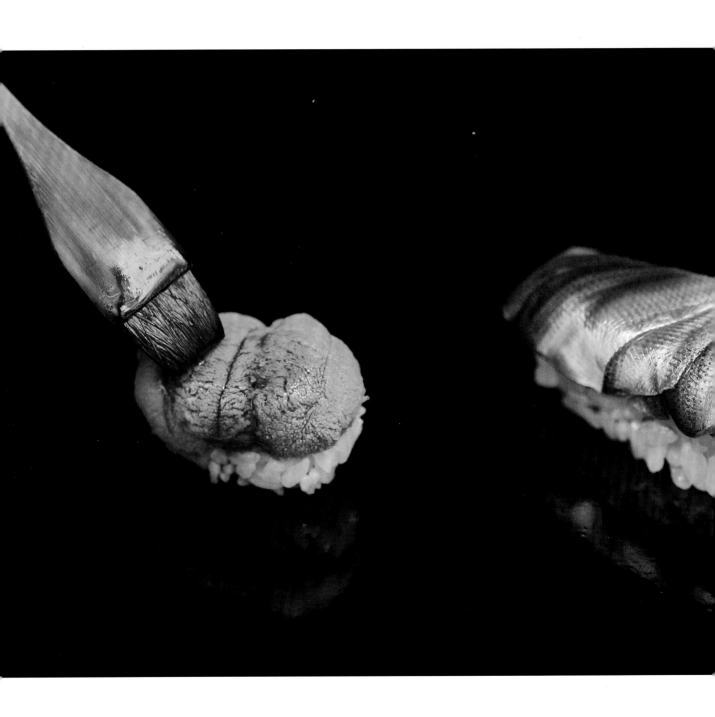

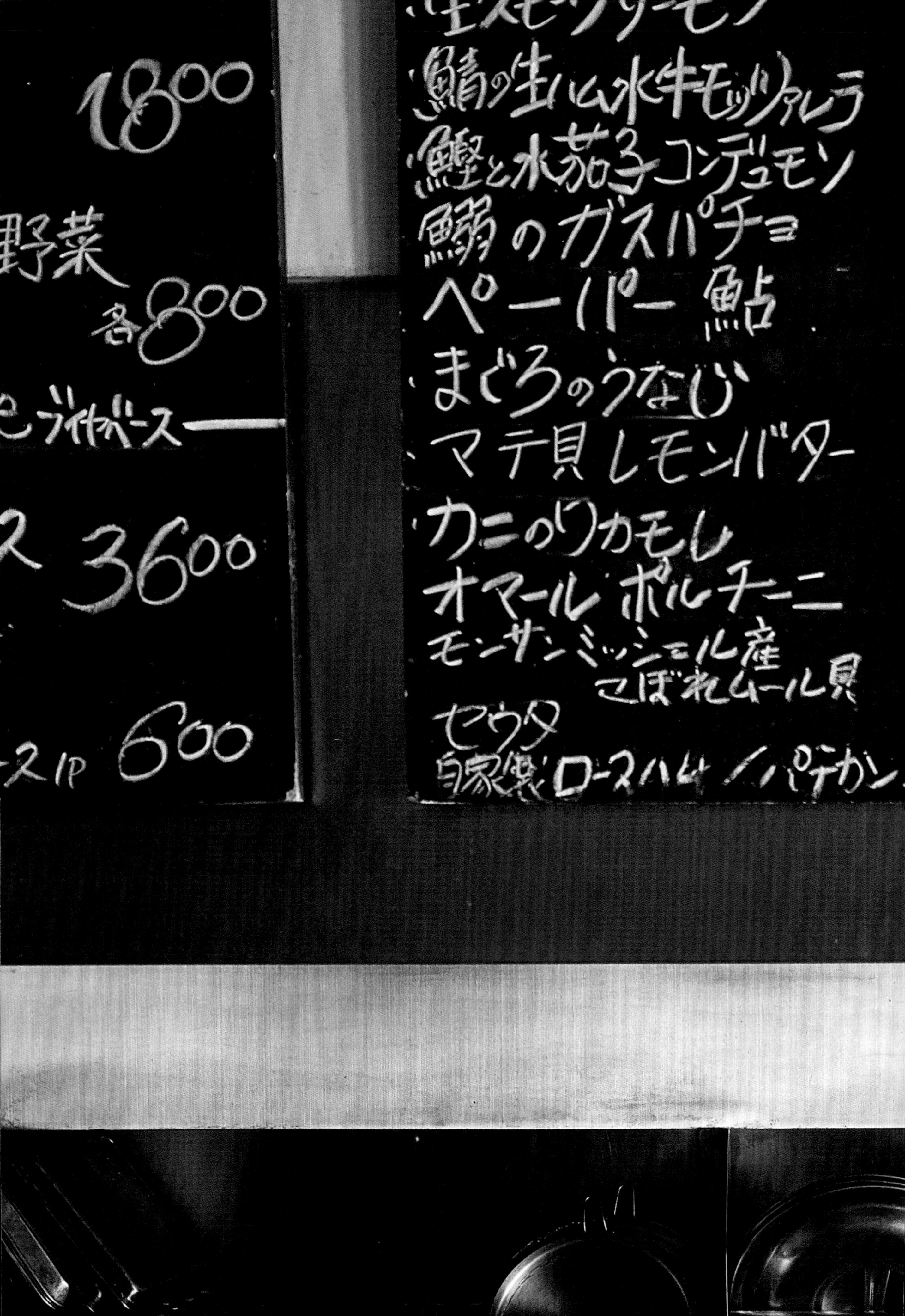

18.00

野菜 各8.00

…ブイヤベース—

…ス 36.00

…ス1P 6.00

生スモックサーモン
鯖の生ハム 水牛モッツァレラ
鰹と水茄子コンデュモン
鰯のガスパチョ
ペーパー鮎
まぐろのうなじ
マテ貝 レモンバター
カニのりかもれ
オマール ポルチーニ
モンサンミッシェル産
　　こぼれムール貝
セウタ
自家製ローズハム／パテカン

カスベのムニエル　3400
あんこうのほっぺ　3600
甘鯛 あさり 青唐　3800
穴子 フォアグラ田楽　3600
牛イチボ ステーキフリット　2000（100g）
ポーク スペアリブ　2800
仔羊背肉のロースト　3000
牛スネのパルマンティエ　3500
パン　500

SATOSHI
KAKEGAWA

ÄTA

FAMILY

HUMANITY

I sit waiting for Satoshi Kakegawa at Äta, his restaurant on the edge of Daikanyama. Looking out the open back windows, I savor green tea accompanied by the sound of chirping birds and the click of the sommelier writing out the day's menu on a chalkboard. Suddenly, like a bolt of electricity, Kakegawa appears. He tries to catch his breath as he removes his backpack, smiling broadly and apologizing profusely for making me wait. His ebullience and excitement are so apparent, the walls of the restaurant can barely contain him.

I notice his *chonmage*-inspired hair (a samurai hairstyle where the hair on top is longer and pulled back) and multiple burn marks on his arms. He is wearing a navy blue boatneck top, Bermuda shorts, and blue Converse shoes, as if he just came from a stroll on a seaside boardwalk.

Kakegawa is a man of sincerity, in love above all with his wife and family. Now thirty-eight, he met his wife in high school and they have four children. Human connection fuels him in the kitchen and in life. He does not believe in frills, airs, or ostentation and favors the basic over the elaborate. His hardworking parents were often absent when he was a child, impacting many of his life choices. Kakegawa's sense of humor and coltish way of being lend him an air of familiarity and amity; I feel as if I have known him a long time.

On a subsequent visit, Kakegawa is more somber and pensive. The moisture in his eyes reflects the window's light as he shares remembrances of Fukushima. He traveled there after the tsunami to help in the recovery before he had his own restaurant. He fed people in need—he listened to them, talked with them, played with their children. This fraternity, sense of purpose, and desire to provide good, simple food for others was the biggest motivation for opening Äta, which means "to eat" in Swedish. He would never have considered naming the restaurant anything else.

The first time I eat at Äta, I sit at the wood counter dotted with an eclectic menagerie of irreverent animal figurines, stacked plates, and a full view of the galley kitchen. To make me laugh, Kakegawa endearingly places a smiling donkey on a surfboard right before me.

After an afternoon together in Kamakura where Kakegawa grew up, he is keen to know what I would like to order. His restaurant is his soul, he tells me. His sincere desire to cook for me and make me happy touches my soul in turn.

INTERVIEW

Why do you cook?

My parents are businesspeople, so from a young age, I had to cook for myself. They were always busy. Since I was ten years old, as a middle child, I cooked with my brothers. We cooked to live really, because my parents were at work. Cooking seemed natural me.

When did you decide to become a chef?

When I was fifteen years old. I also dreamed of traveling and taking photos, but I couldn't trust myself to be good enough at it. I wasn't sure if I could become a successful photographer and eventually support a family. My family is everything to me.

Tell me about your time working at Narisawa.

I applied to Narisawa because I thought it was the best French restaurant in Tokyo at the time. I was sous chef there for three years. It was such an intense time—the *Michelin Guide* had just started in Japan and the World's 50 Best Restaurants list had launched. The concept and artistic philosophy at Narisawa were very strong; it was quite an artistic philosophy. It was more than just a restaurant. I learned a lot about expression.

You seem to have been influenced by your time at Narisawa. Why didn't you decide to open a fine dining restaurant, too?

In 2011 the earthquake and tsunami struck. The disaster affected everything; no one was going out to eat. I had to throw out a lot of food. Meanwhile, everyone was hungry in Fukushima. Here in Tokyo, there was food, but no one wanted to eat out. With this tragedy, I thought a lot about what a chef can do. I wanted to make customers happy. I could no longer agree with the concept of fine dining anymore. I believe eating food should be more simple. I thought about mortality and how we all could have died.

Really, I think the idea many chefs have about food is egotistical. I volunteered up in the Fukushima area. I made curry rice, played with children, talked to people, stayed with them—there was nothing there. It was then that I came up with the idea of Äta and the atmosphere here. I wanted it to be very warm. That sense of humanity and what it means to be human was so strong to me. Everyone was telling me that when they are eating they are happy. People gathered for food and felt things; the people in Fukushima felt relief, they felt normal again.

Why Äta?

Äta means "to eat" in Swedish. It is simple and straightforward. When I opened, I decided not to make it the place where I literally expressed my philosophy. I just wanted to make it a simple place. A chef I knew once asked me, "Are you eating to live or are you living to eat?" I think about this often. I cook for people to live. Let's just eat.

What is your earliest food memory?

Spaghetti *naporitan*. My mom made it for me when I was little. It's Japanese spaghetti. Mom wasn't good at cooking but I loved what she made. She cooked only on Saturday. I remember how hungry I was—I was crying. When Mom served it, I was so happy. It was so delicious!

For you, what does it mean to be Japanese?

I have *bushido* spirit [the way of the samurai, typified by eight virtues]. I'm very hardworking and strict with myself. To live and to work is the same for me. I'm always thinking about the end of my life and what it will look like. How I can live, what I will leave behind.

What do you like most about Tokyo?

I think Tokyo is small. There are so many people in Japan, but the people who make up the different groups in Tokyo like the food or fashion communities really aren't that many. I think of Tokyo as being like the American dream. All kinds of people come to my small restaurant, which is like a microcosm of the world. It's like the Tokyo dream.

If you could share a meal with anyone, who would it be?

Napoleon.

Takafumi Horie, a famous businessman.

My great-grandfather. One hundred years ago, he moved to Canada at the age of fifteen.

What is your favorite word?

Tanoshimu, which means enjoy everything.

SARDINE GAZPACHO

I wanted to make cold tomato soup and a seasonal sardine dish; I really like both dishes and ingredients. I usually create a dish by drawing and painting a picture in my head. For this dish, I created a rough sketch of tomato soup (gazpacho) with hot sardine on top of it. To me, it looked unusual and interesting because I had never seen a whole sardine on top of gazpacho. Then I added the flavor, texture, and temperature, like a painting. The tomato gazpacho and sardine confit is a wonderful flavor combination as well as an unexpected mix of hot and cold.

SARDINE CONFIT

4 sardines, each about 6 inches long, scaled and gutted

Sea salt

1¼ cups extra-virgin olive oil

3 cloves garlic, chopped

1 thyme sprig

1 rosemary sprig

GUACAMOLE

2 avocados, diced

2 tablespoons diced shallot

4 teaspoons freshly squeezed lemon juice

1 tablespoon heavy cream

GAZPACHO

1½ pounds tomatoes, peeled, seeded, and chopped

1½ cups tomato juice

½ cup diced cucumber

½ cup minced yellow onion

Juice of 1 lemon

1 tablespoon extra-virgin olive oil

Sea salt

Tabasco sauce , for seasoning

4 thin slices baguette, crusts removed

Chopped chives, for garnish

SERVES 4

To make the sardine confit, sprinkle the sardines with sea salt, cover with plastic wrap, and chill overnight in the refrigerator.

The next morning, combine the olive oil, garlic, thyme, and rosemary in a small Dutch oven and cook over medium heat until the oil beings to simmer, about 2 minutes. Add the sardines to the pot, lower the heat, and simmer 7 to 8 hours, until completely cooked, head to tail. Transfer the sardine and oil mixture into another container. Set aside.

To make the guacamole, mash together all of the ingredients in a medium bowl or puree in a blender. Set aside.

To make the gazpacho, combine the tomatoes, tomato juice, cucumber, onion, lemon juice, and olive oil in a blender. Set the blender to stir and process for 2-second intervals three times. Set the

blender to mix and process for 20 seconds. Season with salt and Tabasco to taste. Set the blender to puree and process for 30 seconds more. Refrigerator until cold, about 1 hour.

Preheat the oven to 300°F.

Just before serving, remove the sardines from the oil and place on a baking sheet. Warm in the oven for 5 minutes.

Place the baguette slices in the center of four soup bowls, then divide and spoon the gazpacho over the bread. Place 1 tablespoon of guacamole on top of the gazpacho. Place 1 sardine on top of the guacamole in each bowl and sprinkle with chives. Serve right away.

NOTE: You have to start this recipe at least one day ahead. Ask your fishmonger to scale and clean the sardines.

YOSHITERU IKEGAWA

TORISHIKI

PLUCK

TERROIR

Yoshiteru Ikegawa's rolled blue-and-white *tenugui mameshibori* (head scarf) sits perched atop his smooth, tan head. A soul patch dots his chin. His defined jaw, stature, and uniform recall the traditional figures of Edo-period woodblock prints. As he stokes the flames of the grill at Torishiki, his restaurant in Meguro, he admits that he has never been professionally photographed. They only come to photograph the yakitori, he says.

As a *shokunin* (master artisan) who does not profess to being one, Ikegawa believes that yakitori is one of the last remaining "analog cuisines" in Japan. His profound zeal for his craft is reflected in his enthusiasm for his materials: the charcoal and the chickens. As he preps his grill, looking up occasionally to smile, he explains how the odorless charcoal is alive and exudes intense energy both when lit and not lit. The chicken and vegetables absorb this energy during the grilling process, and as such, diners ingest, feel, and benefit from its energy. Dating back to the Edo period, the charcoal is called *kishu binchō-tan* and is from Wakayama Prefecture. It is ebony in color; the raw material is oak and as hard as glass.

I comment about the beauty of a shadow on the wall and Ikegawa smiles, exclaiming his stunned delight that I appreciate such a detail. This is one of the reasons I moved to Japan—to revel in the details with like-minded people.

The chickens Ikegawa serves are descended from French Bresse chickens and a domestic Japanese breed. They come from a farm near Iwate Prefecture, in the heart of the mountains, where they roam the open grassy spaces; the water is pure and the insects plentiful. Ikegawa tried many chickens before choosing this particular breed for Torishiki. They are the healthiest for the human body and have the most umami, he explains.

Ikegawa's very first food memory is of eating yakitori in Tokyo; chicken has always been central to his life. He starts to fan the charcoal, pulling out a large ecru *uchiwa* (fan) from the small of his back. Isegawa begins to grill *tsukune* (ground chicken). He presents glistening skewers to me a few at a time, pacing the meal just as a sushi master would. His discreet attention to the rhythm of the meal makes for a graceful, perfectly timed experience. The finale is *oyako-donburi,* a hearty of bowl of chicken and egg over rice.

As I ready to leave, Ikegawa graciously gives me a bag of *kishu binchō-tan.* I am honored to accept his generous gift so that I can enjoy the charcoal's organic energy long after my meal has ended.

INTERVIEW

Why do you cook?

Yakitori is very important to me; it is a big part of my life. Yakitori places are very local. When I was in elementary school, there was an entire street filled with yakitori vendors, like there used to be in Asakusa [a district in Tokyo]. I would buy one skewer of yakitori as a snack. I liked the smell of the charcoal. You don't really cook yakitori at home, but by buying the yakitori, you can bring the charcoal smell home.

I wanted to be either a yakitori chef, a baseball player, or a high school teacher.

What is it about charcoal that you like so much?

Right now we are in a digital society, but charcoal is the opposite. It's analog. Primitive.

What motivates you?

It's important to me to be in the kitchen. I work about fourteen hours a day. I grill for about eight hours. I train mentally and physically. I need to be in shape. My sense of purpose is my restaurant. I want to protect it, make sure it is successful. When I first started, the restaurant was very local. Now we have reservations from people from all over the world. I couldn't live without yakitori, and I want to share everything I know about yakitori and Japanese culture with my guests.

What is your definition of a *shokunin* (master artisan)?

Someone who puts his soul into what he does. Someone who knows his product so well that it's instinctive. Sometimes customers ask me to make beef or pork yakitori, but I think yakitori should only be chicken. So I don't do it. I think I am not yet a *shokunin*, but each day I work toward it. Every day I learn more.

What is your earliest food memory?

I was about five years old. When my dad finished work, he would go to a typical local *izakaya* with his friends, and sometimes he would bring me. There was always yakitori there. I remember the sauce and how delicious it was.

For you, what does it mean to be Japanese?

Okuyukashisa [telling someone something without saying it]. We are generally not good at self-promotion. Maybe something can be said just with energy or body language, without speech. This is beautiful to me. In old movies, actors would act without saying much. The use of silence is also quite Japanese to me. Timing, or *ma*—whether at a restaurant or a Kabuki performance. Knowing when to present food is very important. It should not be intrusive. We know when to serve and when not to serve.

Counter dining is wonderful for this reason. I always tell my staff to use their five senses: smell, sight, taste, touch, and sound. For example, if a customer spills something, it is up to us to anticipate her needs before she asks for help. Some customers tell me I have eyes in the back of my head.

If you could share a meal with anyone, who would it be?

My wife and my parents. There is no one who is famous who I am interested in meeting.

What is your favorite word?

Honesty.

What is one of your favorite films?

The Godfather, for the family love. My staff is also my family. The relationships portrayed and the strong and intense spirit of the film are appealing to me.

CHICKEN AND EGG OVER RICE (OYAKO-DONBURI)

Invented about 130 years ago here in Tokyo, oyako-donburi is also known as Oyakodon, which literally means "parent and child donburi"—the parent and child is the chicken and the egg. Donburi is a rice bowl dish, usually made with simmered meat, fish, or vegetables that is served over rice with a thin layer of lightly cooked egg on top.

OYAKO SAUCE

1 cup chicken broth

½ cup plus 1 tablespoon mirin

½ cup plus 1 teaspoon soy sauce

5 tablespoons sugar

OYAKO-DONBURI

2 boneless skinless chicken thighs or 1 boneless skinless chicken breast, cut into bite-size pieces

3-inch piece of leek, chopped

½ cup steamed Japanese short-grain white rice

Shredded nori, to top the rice

2 eggs, separated and lightly whisked in two bowls

Fresh mitsuba or cilantro leaves, for garnish

SERVES 1

To make the oyako sauce, combine all of the ingredients in a sauté pan and bring to a boil over medium heat for about 5 minutes, until the sugar has dissolved and the sauce has thickened. Remove from the heat and pour into a bowl.

To make the oyako-donburi, add the chicken and leek to the oyako pan or a 6-inch nonstick sauté pan with ¼ cup oyako sauce and cook over low heat. When the mixture starts to boil, turn the chicken to cook evenly and simmer 5 minutes, turning occasionally, until cooked through or to your desired doneness.

Meanwhile, put the rice in a bowl and layer the nori over the top, making sure that the rice is completely covered. Keep warm.

Pour the egg whites in a thin stream onto the chicken in a circular pattern. Separately, add the egg yolks in four distinct places around this circle. All of the egg whites and egg yolks should be used. Shake the pan and tilt it a bit right and left for about 6 seconds to spread out the ingredients, allowing them to cook equally. Make sure that the egg does not touch the sauté pan's surface, which would cause it to overcook. Cover the pan, raise the heat to high, and cook for about 1 minute, until the egg has cooked through. Uncover the pan and quickly transfer everything to the bowl with the rice by sliding it out of the pan. Garnish with a mitsuba leaf and serve right away.

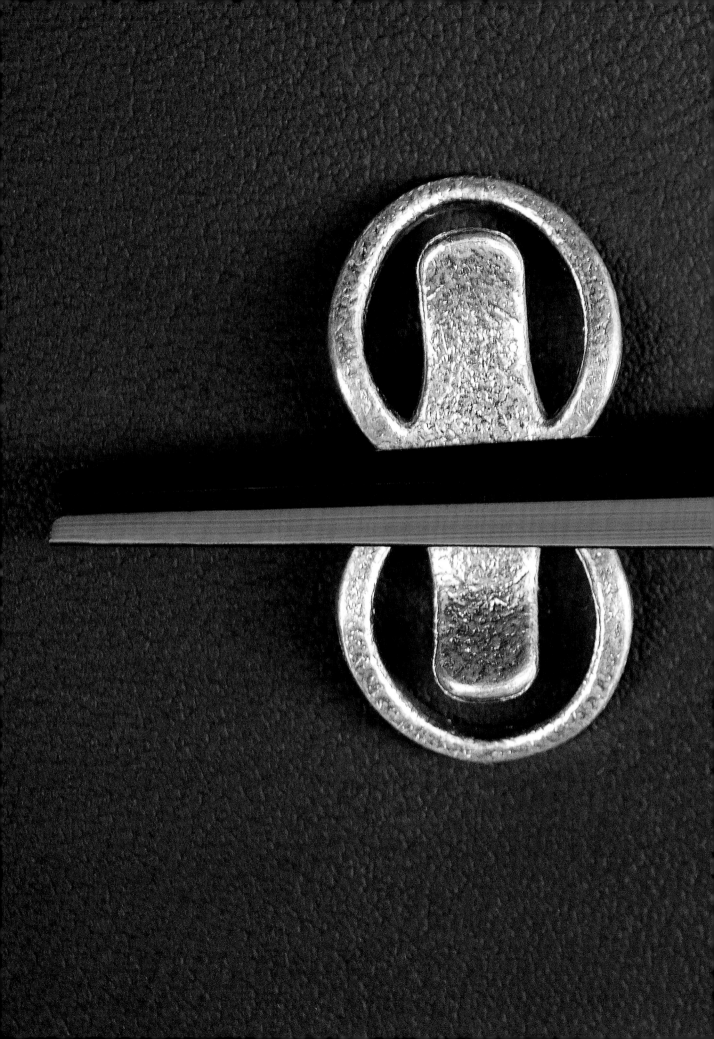

YOSHIAKI
TAKAZAWA

TAKAZAWA

RIGOR

SOPHISTICATION

I enter through a door framed in white neon and climb a flight of stairs to Takazawa. Engraved in the bannister is an excerpt from a poem by American poet Joyce Kilmer: "I think that I shall never see a poem as lovely as a tree. Poems are made by fools like me, but only God can make a tree."

The interior is small, urbane, and rich in dark hues, except for a striking illuminated central steel island that resembles a hypermodern altar—this is where Yoshiaki Takazawa holds court. Members of his team occasionally appear from behind an obscured black door to provide an ingredient or briefly assist, but by and large Takazawa is out there on his own, controlling every aspect of service. His wife, Akiko, is a constant and courteous presence who explains the simultaneously cerebral and whimsical dishes.

Dining at Takazawa is based on the Japanese tea ceremony. With only five tables and no counter, each guest can enjoy Takazawa's tremendous focus during service. There is no chitchat, though he occasionally comes from behind the island to present a dish himself. He is an intense, distinguished, and precise maestro. His longish salt-and-pepper hair is meticulously set in place so as not to fall in front of his eyes. His goal is to host his guests with originality and sophistication, in his clever, contemporary way.

Although Takazawa seems businesslike during service, there is a playfulness and inventiveness to his luxurious dishes, a hallmark of molecular gastronomy. One dish, Fish and Chips, features edible paper; another called Candle Holder presents foie gras in a glass pot with a crème brulee–like glaze, resembling a scented candle; and another is Ratatouille, a bite-size vegetable terrine that recalls a mosaic of multicolored jewels. While Takazawa's style of cuisine is distinctly global, it is steeped in Japanese soul.

When I taste his dishes, I recall textures, colors, scents, and vistas from Vietnam, Russia, England, and Italy—all in one tour-de-force meal. Interestingly, Takazawa never trained abroad, though he embraces countless international themes and techniques with bravura and expertise.

After service, we sit to chat in his nearby lounge, Takazawa Bar, and I discover he speaks English. He opens up and conveys a much more relaxed demeanor outside of service hours, especially as he lovingly recalls his grandmother. I learn that she cultivated his imagination and love of food early on. For all the restaurant's rigor, worldly cultivation, and panache, it is the simple memories of time with his grandmother, visiting gardens and enjoying food together, that are at Takazawa's core.

INTERVIEW

Why do you cook?

My parents had a restaurant in Koenji. I grew up in their kitchen and had a number of responsibilities. But I wanted to be a Japanese chef for my grandmother. My parents were very busy. Every day after elementary and junior high school, I would go home to my grandmother and she would cook for me. She would sometimes bring me to the park, like Jindai Botanical Park in Mitaka [western Tokyo]. To this day, whenever I see flowers I think of her. I loved her and loved being with her.

What motivates you?

When I graduated from culinary school, I was at the top of the class. At graduation, I was to have received the best award, but the teachers didn't like that I would correct them. Only one teacher liked me. They said I was a bit too blunt and honest. They told me I wouldn't be a successful chef, but I wanted to prove them wrong.

What is your earliest food memory?

When I was a kid, about four or five, I was playing with some cooking tools, like a veggie slicer, and I cut my finger. I was cutting a cucumber with a mandoline and didn't realize I was cutting my finger.

For you, what does it mean to be Japanese and how do you think growing up in Japan informs your style?

Nowadays I have many chances to go to other countries to meet many foreigners. After we travel and come back to Japan, I always feel that Japan is convenient, comfortable, and peaceful, with very tasty food as well.

Details are very important, and so is an interest in learning. In the restaurant industry in Japan, we are educated by older chefs who are very strict. Now, however, this is a changing a bit.

We respect the seasons and ingredients. Because of my grandmother, I understand the seasons. I want the customer to understand where they are eating, what they are eating, and why they are eating it at that particular moment in time.

What is tough about your industry?

Working in the restaurant industry is very hard work, with long working hours. Chefs' lives are shortened once they become head chef. It's a stressful life physically and mentally. We are like athletes. But I would like to change this. I'd like staff to stay longer and stick with things longer; they are impatient. We need to change the dynamic in society, where cooks get low pay for long hours.

What is your favorite word?

Passion.

TAKAZAWA

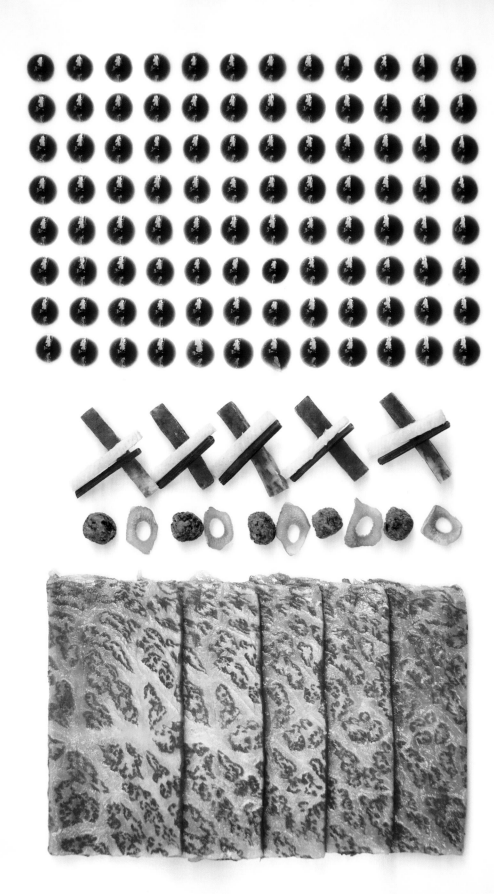

TAKAZAWA SASHIMI

Classic sashimi dishes are traditionally simple sliced fish with soy sauce. I wanted to do it in a more modern way with a twist. So I played with and updated the presentation to make it a bit more unexpected.

LEEK OIL

1 tablespoon coarsely chopped leeks

4 teaspoons olive oil

3½ tablespoons soy sauce

3½ tablespoons tamari, at room temperature

1½ teaspoons agar agar powder

1 red daikon radish, cut into 12 bâtonnets

2 chives, cut into 12 bâtonnets, plus ½ teaspoon chopped fresh chives

12 bâtonnets fresh peeled ginger, plus 2 tablespoons grated ginger, from about 1 piece fresh ginger

4 cloves garlic, peeled

10 ounces sashimi (any seasonal, high-quality Wagyu beef or sushi-grade fish) or 20 slices, each about 3 by 1½ by ½ inches

SERVES 4

To make the leek oil, crush the leeks in earthenware mortar and pestle. Mix in the olive oil and continue crushing until coarsely ground, not smooth. Set aside.

In a small bowl, stir together the soy sauce, tamari, and agar agar powder until the mixture thickens enough so that a drop of it on a plate will keep its shape. Decorate a serving platter large enough to fit all of the sashimi with 96 dots of this mixture in 8 lines on the top of the platter.

Arrange the radish, chives, and ginger bâtonnets in small crosses in the center of the plate.

In a small bowl, stir together the grated ginger and chopped chives until it clumps into little balls, then place them on the platter next to the vegetable bâtonnets. Slice the garlic ⅛ inch thick. In a small pan, cook the garlic in the leek oil over medium heat, stirring frequently, until the garlic is light brown and crisp, about 15 minutes. Transfer the garlic chips to a paper towel to absorb any extra oil, then place them in between the balls of grated ginger and chives.

Just before serving, arrange the slices of sashimi on the platter below the other ingredients.

NOTE: A *bâtonnet* cut is a vegetable cut into batons or sticks, in this case 1 by ⅜ by ⅛ inches.

PURITY

REVERIE

"I want to give my customers my heart." Hayato Takahashi and I pause, sitting in silence, allowing his response to my question, "Why do you cook?" to linger.

Takahashi is highly unusual—he is a restaurant of one. There is no sous chef, no wait staff, no sommelier, no dessert chef, no dishwasher. Takahashi *is* the restaurant Pellegrino. It is as if he hosts an intimate group of six at his home every night. His level of exactitude is both wondrous and inspiring, the purest expression of respect for the tradition, technique, and ingredients of Italy, particularly the city of Parma, where he lived and worked for one year.

I do not think there is a chef who cooks and runs a restaurant quite like Takahashi, making everything 100 percent from scratch and completely on his own. The dining room is the kitchen; each of the chairs at the three tables of two face him. The dining experience is entirely devoid of artifice or theatrics, forgoing the traditional restaurant structure and dynamic.

At Pellegrino, nothing comes between the diner and the food; this is deeply personal dining. Takahashi is remarkably attuned to every detail, even beyond the food itself. The evening's music, for example, is selected with as much care as each ingredient. Every appliance—imported from Italy, of course—is out in the open for all to see. If you are looking for a flashy dining experience, this restaurant is not for you.

Takahashi is a gentle yet intense soul; when he speaks, he does so with an almost constant grin. His eyes dart around searching for his carefully chosen words as he admits that he likes things done just so.

Recounting his experiences working at Trattoria Le Viole near Parma, Takahashi lights up. He has an especially deep reverence for prosciutto and its place in Italian culture, equating it with sushi's stature in Japan. A large red prosciutto slicer is the focal point at Pellegrino. Takahashi is a virtuoso as he attentively unwraps a whole prosciutto di Parma, preparing it for slicing. He is entirely engrossed in his task; I feel that if I were to speak, he wouldn't hear me. Takahashi places the large leg on the Italian-made slicer and pushes the blade back and forth. All I can hear is the swishing sound of the blade cutting the prosciutto. Delicate slices fall into Takahashi's left hand, and he gingerly places them, one at a time, on a white porcelain plate. The distinctive fragrance of prosciutto permeates the room. It is not until Takahashi offers me the plate that he awakens from his trance.

As we share memories of eating prosciutto in Italy, he describes his first taste as a revelation. It was "scrumptious," he says with a mischievous grin.

I mention how my grandfather enjoyed eating prosciutto with figs, and Takahashi meanders to his refrigerator without saying a word. He presents me with two deep red figs and carefully slices each one, half peeled, half not, offering both to me with slices of prosciutto. We stand together savoring these morsels of happiness and remembrance.

I spend hours with Takahashi at Pellegrino, high on his tenderness and talent. His dishes are the closest thing to the finest, authentic trattoria dining, short of a trip to Italy. He absorbed an extraordinary amount during his year working in Italy, a place where he left part of his heart.

I watch as Takahashi makes plump ravioli for his *brodo*, a broth with a touch of sherry that cooks for twelve hours. He offers me a spoonful, and as I savor the first drop, he says with his unabating grin, "I want to be a chef for the rest of my life."

INTER VIEW

When did you become a chef?

It was when I was in Auckland, New Zealand, that I decided I would become a chef. At first I was a dishwasher, but then I started doing more. I learned about vegetables and tempura and many of the other cooked dishes. I met my future wife there, and we came back to Shikoku together. I brought my résumé and walked from restaurant to restaurant handing it out. My plan was to work at an Italian restaurant! My boss in Auckland always said to me, "Italian food looks simple, but it is very hard to do well." He also felt that there were many similarities between Japanese food and Italian food.

Why did you choose to go to Parma?

I wanted to go to Parma to learn to like prosciutto because it is so culturally important in Italy, and Italian restaurants in Japan do not generally serve good prosciutto. This was my first time in Italy. Emilia-Romagna is beautiful—the landscape, the houses, the terra-cotta colors. I loved it. When I saw this for the first time, I thought how Italian it all looked!

At my first meal in Emilia-Romagna at Le Viole, the chef served prosciutto di Parma with melon and Parmigiano-Reggiano, Lambrusco, and bread. It was a huge portion. This was lunchtime. I was amazed. It was beautiful. Awesome. Scrumptious. When I ate the prosciutto, my heart exploded. The quality was unbelievable—it was like nothing I had ever tasted before. Every day, I would ask the chef how to make *cucina parmigiana*. I wanted to learn Parma cuisine. I learned how to make chicken broth with Lambrusco, and pasta by hand like *farfalle al ragù di Parma* [chopped prosciutto, red and yellow peppers, basil, white wine, fresh tomato, *salsiccia*, Parmigiano]. I was so happy there.

What made you so happy?

It felt like my home. The chef taught me everything. Because I stayed in Parma the whole time, I know only this part of Italy well. I am Japanese, so I can't learn about all Italian food. Most people seem to want general knowledge about many parts of Italy, but I specialized in Parma food. I realized I wanted to open a restaurant with Parma food that is also unique to me, with a bit of my influence, too. I could have stayed longer—my visa would have been extended. But I wanted to come back and open my own restaurant in Tokyo.

What is your earliest food memory?

I remember my mother's cooking in Niigata. She cooked a lot of Western, European things, but not much Italian food. She made pot-au-feu, buffalo wings, and pork chops with pineapple. I didn't always like these things, but they were interesting.

Tell me about the importance of music in your life.

When I was a teenager, I discovered I loved punk. I couldn't play an instrument. I still like punk music, but really, I appreciate all music. My choice of music in the restaurant is very important. It changes the whole dining experience. I do not play punk music during service; I play minimal slow music, ambient music. My food is gentle but my concept is radical. So I don't need to play punk music during service; it would overwhelm the dining experience. Punk music is strong and pure and not complicated or fancy, like I am.

If you could share a meal with anyone, who would it be?

I would like to meet Versus the World [an American punk band] and Plus/Minus [an American indietronica band], perhaps also Shutoku Mukai [a musician].

What is your favorite word?

Prosciutto.

ROAST LAMB WITH EGGPLANT PUREE AND FALL TRUFFLES

This dish is an earthy one, which beautifully expresses some of the most seminal elements of nature in the fall. The tender lamb pairs so well with the perfumed truffles and sweet eggplant, conveying the poignancy of Italian terroir.

2 small round eggplants (marunasu) or 1 globe eggplant, halved

Sea salt

1½ pounds Frenched lamb rack

1 tablespoon unsalted cultured butter

2 ounces fresh brown or black fall truffle

SERVES 4

Preheat the oven to 400°F.

Heat a dry sauté pan over medium heat. Add the eggplants and sear until brown on both sides, about 5 minutes per side. Transfer to a baking dish and roast for 1 hour, until the eggplant is softened and most of the liquid has cooked out. Remove from the oven and let cool. Lower the oven heat to 325°F to cook the lamb.

When the eggplant is cool enough to handle, peel and put into a blender. Add a pinch of sea salt and puree for just a second until just blended.

Place the unseasoned rack of lamb in an ovenproof dry sauté pan or roasting pan, place in the oven, and roast for 6 minutes. Remove from the oven and let rest for 2 minutes. Flip the rack and roast for 5 minutes more. Remove from the oven and let rest again for 2 minutes.

In a dry frying pan, sear the rack of lamb over high heat, until browned on all sides, about 5 seconds per side. Immediately season with salt. Leaving the lamb juices in the pan, transfer the lamb to a platter and let rest.

Add the butter to the juices in the pan and cook over medium heat, stirring to combine, until the butter melts.

Place a big spoonful of eggplant puree in the center of a serving plate. Carve the lamb into ½-inch ribs and arrange on top of the eggplant. Spoon the lamb juices on top and shave the truffle over everything. Serve immediately.

SPAGHETTI AI RICCI DI MARE

When I think about what inspires me to create a dish, I honestly can't think of any one single source. What I cook and what I create comes from a desire to express myself. My dishes come from personal experiences and life lessons, like living in Parma, paired with my desires and hopes for each dish. It is impossible for me to live life solely focused on cooking. The thoughts and different cultures around me affect me, subtly changing me each day.

2 tablespoons coarse sea salt

1 pound spaghetti, such as Martelli brand

1 vine-ripened tomato, cut into ½-inch cubes

5 teaspoons salted cultured butter

8 ounces uni (sea urchin)

SERVES 4

In a pot, bring 3 quarts water and the sea salt to a boil. Add the spaghetti to the boiling water and cook about 6 minutes, until al dente.

Put the tomato and butter in a large bowl. When the pasta is ready, drain it and immediately add it to the bowl with the tomato. Add the uni and mix gently to incorporate the ingredients. Transfer to serving plates and serve immediately.

KAN
MORIEDA

SALMON &
TROUT

FREEDOM

FUN

Thirty-year-old Kan Morieda wears round black glasses reminiscent of I. M. Pei; they give his boyish face a vaguely retro look and a slight quirkiness that suits his jovial personality. He is tall with a refreshingly goofy and good-natured energy. His thick hair remains standing after he runs his fingers through it. He giggles often and is easy to talk to. His restaurant, Salmon & Trout, opened with friend and business partner Shion Kakizaki, is like Morieda himself—warm, welcoming, and rule free. This is a restaurant to hang out in, not just to eat in; hours pass in its cozy glow before you realize it. There are no chef's whites to be found here, no serious self-regard or pursuit of awards and stars. I see a single T-shirt folded on a shelf, an illustration of a fish coming out of a banana and the words "Think Outside the Box" emblazoned across the front. Music from a Sufi rock group plays in the background.

Morieda's informal style is creeping into the food scene in Tokyo. Young chefs like him are liberated by their greater awareness of the culinary world outside Japan and the possibilities this knowledge offers. Conformity is a concept that makes Morieda bristle.

Intriguingly enough, Salmon & Trout is also a bicycle restoration and repair shop called SO!! where the sommelier and DJ space doubles as the reception area for the bike business. The hanging bicycles are not intentional design elements, though they do add even more whimsy to the eclectic space, which is full of found objects from secondhand shops and friends' homes. Even the name Salmon & Trout has an unexpected explanation—it actually means "gout" in East London cockney rhyming slang.

Morieda did not grow up in a traditional Tokyo household. His father, a self-dubbed eccentric, is a photojournalist and food photographer, who recognized early on that his son was interested in food. As a twelve-year-old boy, Morieda was already critiquing the use and type of salt on the chicken when out for yakitori with his dad. Because he was exposed to the artists and other creative people—both Japanese and foreign—who often visited his parent's home, out-of-the-box ideas were valued and encouraged. Absent were the rules, strong customs, and behavioral expectations that others in Japan absorb as children. Morieda is proud to be an outlier, an open and easygoing free spirit.

INTERVIEW

Why do you cook?

I played beach volleyball from seventeen to twenty years old, and I played in Australia for one year. My coach was a famous beach volleyball player who won at the Olympics, Julien Prosser. I liked volleyball a lot; there was more time to play in Australia than in Japan. But my father wanted me to go to Sydney to work at Tetsuya's with his good friend, legendary chef Tetsuya Wakuda—this was the primary reason for going. Ever since I was twelve years old, Tetsuya and my dad had planned for me to go work with him because they noticed how much I liked food.

If you had to describe your food, what would you say?

Japan has a long history of adapting foods from other cultures. Things like fermentation—miso, shoyu—originated in China. The concept of sushi originated in Vietnam and Thailand. My father wrote about this in a book called *Food in Southeast Asia*. Likewise, I'm trying to incorporate influences from Southeast Asia as well as what I learned at Tetsuya's into my cooking. For example, in my tartar sauce, I put the insides of the *ayu* [sweetfish]. That is what makes my take on fish and chips different—no one uses *ayu* in England.

I also use a lot of local ingredients with European ideas. The mozzarella I use is from Shibuya, not Italy—the milk is from Kiyose and Higashikurume. And there's nectarine and fermented tomato in my caprese, too. Fermented tomato, again, is a Southeast Asian concept. I like to twist dishes and change them. My business partner, Shion Kakizaki, is a food journalist and *caviste* [person in charge of a wine cellar], and we have the same vision.

For you, what does it mean to be Japanese?

Uniqueness is not considered a good thing. Kids in school have to follow all these rules and are just told to do things because they have to do them. Your average young person likes a leader and won't question anything. They all want to be the same.

But there a lot of unique of people walking around Tokyo.

Yes, at an older age this can change—when they get the courage to express themselves. Some people start in their late teens or even as older adults. I don't think it's good to be like everyone else. My dad is unconventional, which is odd for Japan. He has unique, quirky friends. I want to be like that. I didn't want to be a salaryman. I like creative people because I am a creative person. My dad was creative, but school wasn't like this.

If you could meet anyone in public life, who would it be?

Usain Bolt. I think he's really cool. He's taller than I am. I want to take a photo with him!

What is your favorite word?

Can I give you a whole sentence? I like the saying "Before you embark on a journey of revenge, dig two graves."

What is one of your favorite films?

Godzilla. Godzilla is a symbol of earthquakes and other natural disasters. Japanese people always have the idea that we will lose everything someday because of natural disasters . . . it's always in the back of our minds. We deal with difficulty. And we find solutions. It's a complex system.

NECTARINE AND BURRATA SALAD WITH FERMENTED TOMATO JELLY

I like to combine ingredients and ideas from different cultures. Of course, burrata is an Italian cheese, but the idea of fermenting tomatoes comes from Southeast Asia. I thought it would give the dish a twist. Tomatoes are a fruit, so the nectarine just added extra sweetness.

FERMENTED TOMATO JELLY

10 large tomatoes on the vine, with leaves

2 tablespoons sea salt

2 gelatin sheets

SALAD

¼ nectarine

6 cherry tomatoes

4 ounces fresh burrata

1 tablespoon extra-virgin olive oil

4 nasturtium leaves

¼ cup purslane

12 grains of salt

¼ teaspoon fresh black soft peppercorns, chopped (3 or 4 peppercorns)

SERVES 2

To make the jelly, remove the tomatoes and leaves from the vine. Puree the tomatoes and then put the tomatoes, their leaves, and the sea salt into a ziplock bag, seal and shake to incorporate, and let sit for 3 to 5 days at room temperature to ferment. You will know when it is ready when the bag has puffed up.

Strain the mixture through a filter (such as a coffee filter) overnight to allow the juice to come out. (Do not force through a sieve.) The next morning, throw away the puree (or use for something else) and transfer the juice to a bowl.

Fill a small bowl with cold water, dip the gelatin sheets into the water, and soak for 5 minutes.

Pour 10 percent of the tomato juice into a pot and bring to a boil over medium heat. Turn off the heat. Add the gelatin sheets and mix. Add the rest of the tomato juice and mix well. Refrigerate for 2 hours.

To make the salad, slice the nectarine and cut up the cherry tomatoes and burrata into large bite-size pieces and combine them in a medium serving bowl. Add 2 tablespoons of the fermented tomato jelly and the olive oil to the bowl, and toss until evenly coated.

Garnish and season the salad with the nasturtium, purslane, salt, and peppercorns. Serve right away.

NOTE: This recipe requires three days' advance preparation. Fresh black peppercorns are sold on the vine or in a jar.

FUMIE TAKEUCHI

SUSHI TAKE

AUDACITY

SELF-RELIANCE

I arrive fifteen minutes early to meet Fumie Takeuchi. The door to Sushi Take is slightly ajar, and I spy her organizing, dashing to and fro behind the counter. Blaring pop music emanates from her laptop, which dominates the otherwise quiet third floor of this unremarkable Ginza building. I patiently wait. At five minutes to three, the music stops. I take that as my cue to present myself.

Takeuchi's sleepy eyes are expressive; her face is makeup free. She sees me at the door and nods slightly, indicating that I can enter. Timid but welcoming with an infectious smile, Takeuchi is not only one of Japan's few female chefs but also one of the only female sushi chefs, historically an exclusively male profession. As she greets me, I notice her raw, rough hands reflecting her years of hard work butchering fish.

Takeuchi is simultaneously reticent yet curious about my interest in her. She explains, in a mix of Japanese and English, that she chose to be a sushi chef because sushi is honest; it is impossible to hide anything. At eighteen years old, she left Japan, dissatisfied with her country. She waited tables and cleaned rooms at a London backpackers' hotel, where she learned more about herself and the world. When she returned to Tokyo, she realized that she loved sushi even more than music and her other strong interest, mixology. After several serendipitous meetings with a sushi chef at Tsukiji Market, Takeuchi was accepted as an apprentice and mentored by an *oyakata* (master), someone she reveres to this day. She proudly declares that she did not inherit her *sushi-ya* (sushi restaurant) from her father, as many sushi chefs do. She opened it herself.

There are deeply entrenched beliefs and traditions in Japanese culture as to why women have never made good sushi chefs. It was said that the size and temperature of their hands negatively affects the fish and that their makeup (the assumption was that all women wear makeup) interferes with their sense of smell. Stereotypes and sexist views are slowly changing. Takeuchi's male peers recognize her determination and disregard for sexist norms, and in large part consider her one of their own, a skilled Edo-style sushi chef. One of her colleagues marveled that she must have extremely strong character. This is not easy work, he told me.

Years ago, Takeuchi shaved off her long hair, partly for the dramatic change and partly to respect the hygienic standards expected of sushi chefs. It was also in keeping with the honesty behind sushi, the sense of not hiding anything. In a country where gender roles are entrenched and female chefs

are rare, she is an anomaly and she knows it. This is not something she touts or asserts, it is just who she is. Takeuchi never wanted to do what is expected of girls. Only what she expects of herself is important. This is assertive and bold for an otherwise reticent role model who, despite her confidence as a chef, worries that she might not be able to live up to my expectations.

Instead, there is no doubt that she does. When I photograph her, I recognize that she is pleased with this new experience, and has somehow already been changed by it. While I have spent time with thirty-one chefs for this book, my interactions with her have been particularly meaningful. She is not just a notable female chef; she is a notable chef.

INTER VIEW

Why did you choose to go to London?

I really wanted to live abroad. At the time, I didn't like Japan. I didn't feel that there were any good things for me here. I just wanted to leave. I had admired places abroad in films and magazines, and I knew that I didn't want to just go on vacation. I didn't have a driver's license, so I thought it would be hard to move to the United States. I thought it would be easier to move to Europe. So I went in 2001.

At first I wanted to go home because I didn't speak English and I was struggling. I decided to go to a back-packers' hotel to ask if there was a job for me. A receptionist there who loved Japan asked on my behalf and got me work there as a cleaner. There was a bar at the hotel, and every day after work, I would go have a drink where I met a lot of people. I can drink a lot. I can drink a whole pint in five seconds. So I made a lot of friends this way.

What was it like for you growing up in your family?

There are so many traditional roles for women here in Japan. My mom used to tell me, "You're a girl. You have to do this, you have to do that; walk three steps behind. You have to dress a certain way." And I didn't like this. My brother didn't have to do these things, so why did I have to. I didn't like that my father didn't help my mother with the housework and I didn't like that my mother felt as if she always had to obey my father and take care of my grandmother. This is also why I wanted to leave the house. I always played with the boys when I was little. I was told by other girls that it was weird that I played with the boys, so I started playing with the girls. I felt pressured to do so.

I didn't want to work for anyone else. At first, I wanted to open a café. I loved cooking for friends at home, and I loved interior design. I went to an *izakaya* to learn some food skills. After London, I went back to my hometown in Aichi Prefecture, but ultimately moved to Tokyo. I went to Tsukiji fish market to study all the fish, and I kept running into a chef buying product for his sushi shop. Eventually he became my teacher. I realized, this is it. This is what I want to do.

I asked the chef if I could be his apprentice, and he said yes. Often chefs say no to apprenticeships; it's very difficult to convince them to say yes. This was very unusual at the time. I was very nervous. My teacher needed to ask his master to get permission to teach me. His master said that women are strong and work hard these days. I was twenty-eight at the time, which was quite late to start. My teacher was quite strict with me. I never thought about being a woman in a male-dominated arena. It was just what I wanted to do.

Is it more that women aren't interested in doing this, or is it that men make it hard for them?

I think many women are interested in being chefs, but restaurants almost always say no. Even many customers here don't like seeing female chefs, especially in sushi restaurants. It's like this in sumo culture, too. Historically, we don't have images or references of a woman doing this. It's just not understood.

At first, I didn't understand sushi culture and why it was and is so male or so macho. I entered the sushi business but couldn't understand the men's culture. The master is the most important person. If a Japanese master says something like red is blue, then the men will agree. Women are less likely to agree, I think. I needed to watch *yakuza* movies to understand male culture!

What are the challenges of being a female chef in Tokyo or in Japan in general?

I do believe that in society there are still many traditional and sometimes sexist attitudes—that hasn't changed here yet. The idea of outside and inside [public and private] roles for husbands and wives still exist; even young chefs in their thirties think this way.

I get asked a lot by my relatives, "When are you going to get married?" Customers ask if my sous chef is my husband. They are also very curious to know if I'm married or not. If they find out I'm not married, sometimes customers ask why.

Why do you cook?

I wanted to do something only I can do and wanted to be accepted for what I do. I really enjoy cooking. It's very straightforward. It's important for me to be at the counter, to see my customers. I wouldn't want to be hidden in a kitchen.

For you, what does it mean to be Japanese?

Patience. Honesty in work. We tend to do what is asked of us. Here we hide feelings, which is sometimes difficult for me.

What is your earliest food memory?

Fresh tomatoes. When I was in elementary school, my uncle brought these tomatoes home to eat. I thought, "Wow, what flavor!" I ate one like an apple.

Who do you admire in the food world?

The master of my master of my master. I met him when he wasn't cooking anymore. He was in his eighties at the time. The master said a *shokunin* [master artisan] has to have both sides, male and female, within himself. So he told me that because I am a woman, I needed to learn men's ways of thinking. He grew up with geishas so he knew how women thought. Women can multitask. Men can't; they go step by step. But I have to do things simultaneously.

If you could share a meal with anyone, who would it be?

My master.

My father, who is deceased now.

My master's master.

What is your favorite word?

Shisso, which means simplicity or simple.

What is one of your favorite films and why?

The Godfather: Part II. I like that it's about a family. It reminds me of the relationship between me and my *oyakata* [master].

SUSUMU SHIMIZU

ANIS

DEDICATION

CRAFT

Years ago, on assignment in Nice, I came across a *boucherie* (butcher's shop) with a rotating rotisserie displayed out front. It was filled with at least a dozen herb-covered chickens; the juice from the plump birds dripped onto glistening potatoes at the base. I carefully selected and then savored what was the most flavorful roasted chicken I had ever tasted. The scent of the rosemary, thyme, and garlic has long been imprinted in my memory, as has the tenderness of the chicken's oysters. In the years since, no chicken has compared, until I discover the chicken served at Anis, here in Tokyo.

Chef Susumu Shimizu specializes in meats, game, and fowl, and his roasted chickens are on par with the very best in France. While his focus is literally any meat you could imagine—terrines of foie gras, and *saucisse* (sausage) included—he does not ignore vegetables, which are also integral to his cuisine. He learned much of his technique during his time in Paris, where he worked at L'Arpège with the legendary Alain Passard, and with famed butcher Hugo Desnoyer.

Shimizu is an artisan with a touch of doting grandfather—he is only thirty-nine but has the air of a caring and attentive relative who is keen to see you enjoy the meal he has prepared. He is deeply in love with his craft, his product, and the ritual of preparing a meal. From his open kitchen, he is eager to see me enjoy his food; a proud smile appears on his face when I acknowledge his gaze and nod in approval.

Anis is cozy and rustic, reminiscent of a country restaurant; the aroma of roasted meats wafts through the space. Shimizu works predominantly at a *teppan* (griddle), where he browns, cooks, braises, and breaks down his meats for hours on end. The chicken takes four to five hours, and is attentively turned from side to side to side; it never goes into the oven. His knife skills are impressive; Shimizu carves with unprecedented focus and surgical dexterity, pausing occasionally to wipe his hands on the towel thrown over his shoulder.

Once a month, Shimizu hosts specials dinners at Anis, called Meatings, endless courses of meats—beef, boar, venison, pork—for his regulars. I attend one of these gatherings during the Awa Odori dance festival, when colorful dance teams parade by his restaurant throughout the meal. With the din of the beating *taiko* drums and voices of the crowd outside, I watch Shimizu prepare his meats with tremendous focus. Completely engrossed, he pauses only briefly to ask in French: "Are you hungry?"

INTERVIEW

Why do you cook?

At first, I studied to become an engineer, but found that the life it would have given me would have been too predictable. I could see what I was going to become—everything was laid out in front of me. Food was much more mysterious and exciting, and I always loved to eat.

What motivates you?

I never talk about food or cooking, or think too hard about what motivates me. Anything in daily life can inspire me, a passerby, even the wind.

What or who inspired you to become a chef?

My father always liked to cook, which wasn't typical at the time in Kyushu, where I grew up. Women cooked but men didn't. So the fact that he cooked made it seem natural to cook myself.

What is your earliest food memory?

Celery and sausage soup on the weekends when I was about six years old. It was quite European and different than the food my mother made daily. It was simple yet luxurious to me and seemed fancy at the time. Celery is not a Japanese ingredient, so it was also exotic.

Who do you admire in the food world?

I admire Alain Passard. I cooked in his kitchen for two years and I was amazed by the way he cooks, so pure and natural, not rigid and superprecise as in some of the other three-star kitchens. While many chefs at the time were using foam and liquid nitrogen, trying to copy El Bulli, Passard was on the opposite end of the spectrum. He was doing simple and natural cooking in such a free way.

For you, what does it mean to be Japanese?

I don't know. I don't think that I am typically Japanese. When I lived in France, I did not miss Japan, but I did learn more about myself and others. I learned that in Europe it is more about oneself—that people, that chefs, are perhaps more focused on themselves. In Japan, we are like turnips. We go with everything in the kitchen—everything! We enhance the other ingredients, perhaps support them, but we don't dominate the other ingredients. Same with people; we are used to thinking about others and what they need. We often put ourselves second.

The kitchens here in Japan are quiet. Teachers don't say anything. When I was learning in a Japanese kitchen, the teacher said almost nothing. We were supposed to feel what we were to do. A lot of the learning is done in silence. You've noticed that the kitchens are quiet. It's not like in Europe, where the kitchens can be loud and noisy. But I learned that I couldn't be this way in France. I had to be more assertive in order to advance myself. I couldn't stay quiet and say nothing, because then I would be thought of as a pushover. So I learned to talk more and express myself in Paris. And as soon as I did that, I became more international.

If you could share a meal with anyone, who would it be?

Really, I would just invite my grandmother, son, wife, and parents. Famous people don't interest me at all.

What is your favorite word?

Shokunin [master artisan or craftsman].

YUSUKE
NAMAI

ODE

MUSIC

OPENNESS

No matter the culture, chefs often cite music as the crux of their identity. Sometimes chefs provide a soundtrack—often a bold one—at their restaurants, as a way to convey their personalities beyond the plate.

It is because of music that Yusuke Namai became a chef. He is deeply influenced by the guitar, especially rock and blues. He tells me that Jim Morrison, John Lennon, Jimi Hendrix, and Janis Joplin touch his heart, that Keith Richards is an inspiration. He had been working at a live house (a venue where live music is played) in Chiba Prefecture, playing guitar, and thought he would become a professional guitarist. At the live house, he was often fed, but he couldn't afford to pay for his meals. To compensate management, he began to work in the kitchen. Namai is entirely self-taught; he learned technique from books and from trial and error. He also draws quite well in addition to his musical talent. His artistic sensibility helps him create singular ideas in the kitchen.

What is compelling about Namai's dishes at Ode is the presentation. He conceptualizes monochromatic dishes for distinctive, attention-grabbing plating. He tells me that he doesn't like many colors all together, either in life or on the plate. He prefers one color in different shades. And because he likes modern art, he believes that dishes look more contemporary in one color with little decoration. The look is simple but the taste is complex. One dish, sardines with anchovy meringue, is almost entirely gray on gray—plated on a gray dish, it is an arresting statement. He deceives the diner a bit; by questioning our conditioned perceptions and expectations about what a meringue should be. We are programmed to anticipate that meringue will be sweet and for dessert; but instead, Namai makes it salty, fishy, and gloriously addictive. Eating his meals are surprise forays to a land where things are not necessarily what they seem.

One afternoon after lunch service, Namai brings his guitar to play for me; he is clearly an accomplished musician. As I listen and watch, he fades in and out of another dimension, so focused on the strings and the notes that everything and everyone around him disappears. His desire to evolve, improve, and be more assertive is coupled with a softheartedness and a touch of unawareness of how good his food really is. At Ode, Namai's dishes are as stirring as the music he loves.

INTERVIEW

Did you know you wanted to be a chef when you were little?

I liked the sounds of my mother's cooking, the chopping, the boiling, the frying. They mean *family* to me, because I always heard them growing up. Most chefs talk about their mother's cooking. Even if their fathers were cooks, they never talk about their father's cooking, because it is an old-fashioned way of thinking. They expect mothers to do home cooking for the family.

What is your earliest food memory?

Kuri gohan [chestnut rice] in the fall. Take the skin off the chestnuts, wash the chestnuts, then cook them in the rice. I remember there was also dashi and soy sauce. It was made with sticky rice—half sweet, half regular rice.

There is a concept of outside life and indoor life here in Japan.

Yes, historically. Different members of the family had defined roles. My work life should be separate from my private life. I care about my family a lot. I want to talk about them, but feel embarrassed to do so.

It was interesting, when I went to Finland, I met a chef friend's entire family, his children, even grandparents, on my first visit. We all went to the mountains together. This was unusual for me. It's not that way here in Japan, to meet a whole family. He showed me this open way of being, a different way of thinking.

How did you choose the name Ode?

After Andrea Fazzari tried my cooking at the restaurant where I previously worked, she suggested the name and I was amazed by this. I looked up the word and it is exactly how I want to communicate the feeling behind my cooking, which all starts with music. Basically an ode is a poem that is meant to be sung. I try to communicate something poetic and lyrical through my food; I want the experience to be transporting, akin to what you feel listening to music. My dishes and the dining experience are an ode to food. It's the perfect name. I was so happy when she told me. Thank you, Andrea!

What inspired your style of cooking?

The Michel Bras book; I was surprised and amazed by it. I identified with his philosophy of cooking and the simplicity of the ingredients. I've always liked to draw and so I was also impressed by the artistic composition of his dishes.

What are you expressing on the plate?

The dish should have an element of the unexpected. Mouthfeel is important, and so is having many textures to create a rhythm when my guests are chewing. This is because eating is just like experiencing music. I prefer one color at a time. Let me explain it like this. In the fall, up close there are many colors—yellow, red, orange, brown, black—but from far away, the total of all these colors together looks like just one color, such as red. I focus on this, the one color from afar.

For you, what does it mean to be Japanese?

For me, it means being courteous. I'm not assertive or aggressive. I lack initiative compared with foreigners. People don't stand up for themselves and express their opinions. When abroad, I realize I am not like they are.

If you could meet anyone in public life, who would it be?

Keith Richards, Jim Morrison, Janis Joplin, Jimi Hendrix, Robert De Niro, and Roberto Benigni.

When you eat out, what is your favorite food?

Sushi.

Do you have a favorite word?

I have a favorite sentence:

Jibun ga kawareba minna mo kawaru

"If I change myself, everything around me changes."

SARDINES WITH ANCHOVY MERINGUE

I always try to put a sense of fun and playfulness into my recipes. I like hiding little secrets on the plate to give people that sense of wonder. Diners' reactions to my dishes excite me, and when they ask "What is this?" or "What is hidden inside?" I feel particularly good. In this case, it is a sardine covered with meringue (actually anchovy chips), which are the same color and texture as the plate. Once you remove the anchovy chips, you will find beautiful sardines and mushrooms hiding underneath.

ANCHOVY MERINGUE

2 tablespoons olive oil

Heads and bones from
2 sardines

Pinch of fresh chopped
thyme leaves

5 oil-packed anchovy fillets,
chopped

6 tablespoons heavy cream

2 tablespoons mizuame,
corn syrup, or barley malt syrup

3 egg whites

1 tablespoon powdered
egg whites

½ teaspoon sosa gelespessa
(optional)

SARDINES

2 large fresh sardines, cleaned,
scaled, and filleted

Sea salt

ANCHOVY MAYONNAISE

2 oil-packed anchovy fillets,
minced to a paste

3 tablespoons mayonnaise

1 teaspoon grated
Parmigiano-Reggiano

½ teaspoon red wine vinegar

½ teaspoon extra-virgin olive oil

MARINATED MUSHROOMS

5 tablespoons olive oil

1 clove garlic, chopped fine

2 ounces shimeji mushrooms,
diced

2 ounces maitake mushrooms,
diced

Salt

1 tablespoon raisins

1 teaspoon capers in vinegar

½ teaspoon freshly squeezed
lemon juice

1 tablespoon sherry vinegar

Fresh sorrel leaves, for garnish

SERVES 4

To make the anchovy meringue, warm the olive oil in a sauté pan over medium heat. Add the sardine heads and bones and the thyme, and sauté, applying pressure and lightly breaking with a wooden spatula, until the head and bones come apart, about 5 minutes. Add the anchovies and heavy cream, bring to a boil, and immediately remove from the heat. Pour the whole mixture, bones and all, into a blender and puree for about 3 minutes. Strain through a fine-mesh sieve in case there are any large pieces of bone left.

Transfer the cream mixture to another pot, stir in the mizuame, and continue to cook over medium heat until you reach 210°F measured with a candy thermometer. Maintain that temperature, monitoring it with the thermometer, so that it will bind with the eggs whites in the next step.

In a large bowl, stir together the fresh egg whites, powdered egg whites, and sosa gelespessa, if using. Add the cream mixture to the bowl and stir until combined.

Spread out the mixture in a thin layer on the trays of a food dehydrator set to 151°F and dry for 8 hours. If you do not have a dehydrator, spread the meringue in a thin layer on baking sheet and let sit in a warm, dry place for 24 hours, until dry and brittle. When the meringue is done, break it into small squares the size of a quarter and set aside.

To make the sardines, sprinkle the fillets with sea salt on both sides and let sit for 10 minutes. Rinse the salt off under cold running water, pat dry, and cut into ½-inch slices. Set aside.

To make the anchovy mayonnaise, stir together the anchovies, mayonnaise, Parmigiano-Reggiano, and red wine vinegar. Add the olive oil and stir to combine. Set aside.

To make the mushrooms, heat the olive oil and garlic in a sauté pan over medium heat. When the oil shimmers, add both kinds of mushrooms and stir-fry for about 5 minutes, until the mushrooms are slightly golden in color. Add salt to taste, then add the raisins, capers, and lemon juice to taste. Stir-fry for a few minutes, until the mushrooms are golden brown, adding the sherry vinegar toward the end. Remove from the heat and let cool.

Spread the anchovy mayonnaise onto a serving plate. Place the mushrooms on top of the mayonnaise, then nestle the sardine pieces on top. Garnish with the whole sorrel leaves, then layer pieces of the broken anchovy meringue to cover all of the ingredients. Serve immediately.

NOTE: Have your fishmonger clean, scale, and fillet the sardines but ask them to reserve the head and bones for you, which are used in the anchovy meringue. *Mizuame* is a Japanese sweetener similar to corn syrup or barley malt syrup. *Sosa gelespessa* is a thickening agent that's only necessary if you live in a humid climate.

otofuku↓
マグルマザワ

otofuku↓
スゴマゴイト

YUJI
TANI

HOUSE

DRIVE

INDIVIDUALITY

I cannot help but focus on Yuji Tani's tattooed arms when I meet him at his restaurant, House. In Japan, tattoos generally bear a strong stigma and association with organized crime and criminality. They are not commonly seen, not even in kitchens—the opposite of much of the world, where chefs display their tattoos boldly and with pride. Conventional mores in Japan dictate keeping tattoos covered in public. When Tani rides the subway, other passengers often avoid him; they even get up and move. Should he appear in magazines in Japan, his tattoos are removed, Photoshopped out of every photo. But none of this fazes Tani; he shrugs it all off. He is comfortable in his own skin and thinks tattoos are cool and artful, an assertion that undoubtedly reflects his strong, independent streak.

Tani regularly trains with the champion welterweight kickboxer, Takayuki Kohiruimaki, at Kohiruimaki's gym in Ebisu. I get a crash course in the sport, watching as boxers pound away, emitting grunts so loud they startle me. The heat in the second-floor gym increases within minutes of the session's start, and the windows fog with condensation. Tani takes up a place in the center of a red mat, dutifully striking his teacher's gloves with focus and effort.

I watch him box and kick rigorously as he tries to resist the inevitable exhaustion that comes from such a demanding workout. What I like about Tani is that he does his own thing. At forty-one, he has ambitious plans for personal and professional evolution. In this time with him, I get a feel for Tani's tenacity. He also takes a moment to wax poetic about New York City.

Tani has visited New York City many times, embracing and admiring its diversity and endless expressions of individuality. For him, New York City is the center of ideas and culture for the world. He feels at home there and values the acceptance and confluence of so many different ethnicities, which do not exist in Japan.

Tani's restaurant, House, feels like a cross between a Provençal country cottage and an urban loft. Bright, airy, and natural, it is bathed in glorious afternoon light, thanks to floor-to-ceiling windows. A wooden deck and garden feature large olive trees and potted plants. In the dining room, basketfuls of fresh produce are on display, as is abundant garlic marinating in olive oil. The open kitchen is a showcase for heavy iron Staub cookware; the mighty black cocotte pot is House's restaurant logo. Here, the feeling is one of casual, breathy ease, of relaxation and individuality. It's a place where you can feel comfortable in your own skin.

INTERVIEW

Why do you cook?

Cooking suits my personality. It's easy for me to concentrate on something if I really like it. I love creating. My mother influenced my cooking style a lot. I think that my food is based on her home cooking. My food expresses my memories and nostalgia.

If you had to describe your food, what would you say it is?

I think it's French/Italian/Japanese food—these days, the lines blur in Japan.

What motivates you?

I want to create an atmosphere that clients and customers can enjoy and that makes them happy. But I am also getting closer to my dream of showing my creativity through food, like an artist. I want people to feel what they feel when they look at a painting or artwork. I am not satisfied with what I am doing now; this motivates me.

It's unusual to see a chef with so many tattoos in Japan, at least tattoos that are out in the open, that are visible. Why did you decide to get them?

I like rock 'n' roll artists like Guns N' Roses and Aerosmith. I just think tattoos are cool. I wanted them when I was in high school. I got my first tattoo at twenty. People at immigration at the airport in New York City would ask as if I was part of the *yakuza* in Japan. I never cared about being judged by others, because I wanted to prove that I don't judge people. If I had a government job, I would have to wear long sleeves all the time.

What is your earliest food memory?

Obanzai [Kyoto dishes made with simple vegetables and seafood native to Kyoto]. I hated it when I was growing up in Kyoto; now I like it!

How do you think growing up in Japan informs your style?

My Japaneseness influences my presentation, even though it is more European. I care a lot about colors. I sometimes decide on ingredients based on the color. I wouldn't combine green vegetables with red sauce for example. I feel that I exist somewhere in the middle, between the two worlds of presentation really, between Japanese and European.

Why do you want to move to New York City?

New York and Tokyo have a similar atmosphere, so I feel at home there. But in New York, there is more respect for individuality. In Tokyo, people are more concerned with unity and rules than they are with identity. There is a higher regard for tradition here. New York is a city where different ethnic groups live together and respect individuality.

If you could share a meal with anyone, who would it be?

Einstein. I don't really like the past, I prefer the future, but I am so impressed by the theory of relativity.

Chef Thomas Keller.

Zinedine Zidane, the soccer champion.

What is your favorite word?

Zen, which means many things, but among them the idea of reverence for nature, for ingredients, and for others.

What is one of your favorite films and why?

The Godfather. I really like the story of the family affection and bonds, but not the violence!

Ms. Ishizuka
Have a good time!

HOUSE

Thank you.

TOMATO, STRAWBERRY, AND BEET SALAD WITH KEFIR MOUSSE

For my dishes and their presentation, I am always inspired by the four seasons and nature, like the sea, mountains, rivers, and forests. I recall my visits to these places and create recipes that reflect how I felt and what I experienced. Color is also of great importance to me. Ultimately, I strive to create my own kind of homey food.

KEFIR MOUSSE

10 ounces goat milk kefir

½ cup heavy cream

BEET COMPOTE

2 cups water

2 tablespoons granulated sugar

Pinch of salt

8 ounces beets, peeled and cut into ¼-inch slices

SALAD

3½ ounces colorful cherry tomatoes, halved

1 pint fresh strawberries, hulled and cut into ¼-inch slices

Salt

2 teaspoons extra-virgin olive oil

1 tablespoon pomegranate seeds

12 colorful edible flowers, for garnish

6 sprigs mint, for garnish

SERVES 2

To make the kefir mousse, line a sieve with parchment paper and set it over a bowl. Pour the kefir into the sieve and leave it overnight to strain.

The next morning, discard the liquid in the bottom of the kefir bowl. In another bowl, whisk the cream with a hand mixer until it forms soft peaks, about 3 minutes. Fold in the strained kefir until combined.

To make the compote, combine the water, sugar, salt, and beets in a pot and bring to a simmer over medium heat. Simmer until a toothpick inserted into a beet slice encounters no resistance, about 10 minutes. Remove from the heat and let the beets cool in the mixture. Drain the beets, reserving the liquid for a sauce. Reserve ¼ cup of the beet compote for the salad and store the rest for another use.

Boil the beet cooking liquid over high heat until it's about one-fifth of the volume. Remove from the heat and let cool. Reserve 2 teaspoons of the sauce for the salad and store the rest for another use.

To make the salad, toss together the tomatoes and strawberries in a large bowl with salt to taste. Place them in a single layer on a serving plate, leaving some space in between the pieces. In the same bowl, stir together the reserved 2 teaspoons beet sauce, the olive oil, and pomegranate seeds, then spoon the mixture over the salad. Dot the reserved ¼ cup beet compote in the spaces between the fruit.

Fill a pastry bag fitted with the 1⁄16-inch tip with the kefir mousse and squeeze about 1 tablespoon of it onto the plate in the spaces between the fruit and beet compote. Garnish the plate with the edible flowers and mint. Serve immediately.

NOTE: You will need to start this recipe at least a day ahead.

KOTARO
MEGURO

ABYSSE

EXUBERANCE

EAGERNESS

Kotaro Meguro is all smiles when he opens the door to greet me. His gelled and tousled auburn hair and strong facial contours are befitting of an anime character or rock star. Wearing a chef jacket seems too conservative for him.

His drive and boundless energy are indisputable. At just thirty years old, Meguro is one of the youngest Tokyo chefs to own a restaurant, and he admits that he is highly competitive. What pushes him each day in the kitchen is the desire to be better than his colleagues and mentors. He is an alum of Quintessence, where he worked alongside the formidable Shuzo Kishida (page 93), with whom he enjoys a true friendship today. His seafood-only restaurant, Abysse, earned its first Michelin star just six months after opening. Upon hearing the news, Meguro took to Facebook, and with a dash of defiance declared that one star was absolutely not enough.

Meguro is a tour de force of conviction and zeal; his dreams can't wait and must be realized now. As the father of two young daughters, he is also open, playful, and accommodating. On Instagram, he shows me photos of his family at birthday parties, ice skating, and grabbing Sunday treats at his favorite bakery. He welcomes me into the kitchen within minutes of my arrival. Perhaps it is his youth, but his lack of rigidity or hesitation is refreshing.

Abysse is a polished, petite space with a prominent bar, walls painted in shades of blue to reflect the water and seafood theme, and a young, efficient staff. I started with a *shirako* (cod milt) fish cracker with hazelnut crumble, followed by a stunning turnip, crab, and fromage blanc creation that was so artfully plated that the couple next to me gasped. A solitary bisque ball exploded in my mouth, with a rush of potent lobster flavor. And for dessert, his elevated reinterpretation of rice pudding—stuffed half-moon pillows of rice with sake and pistachio—was plated in a cascade of pale yellow, lime green, and white. Meguro's dishes were consistently delicate, visually arresting, and even blissful.

Meguro comes out from the kitchen to see me. With his usual bright smile, he is keen to know what I liked most. With a meal like that, I tell him that there is no doubt he is on track to realize each and every one of his dreams.

INTERVIEW

Why do you cook?

My grandfather was a chef in Shinbashi; he had his own *kappo* [traditional Japanese restaurant] there. I really, really loved my grandfather, especially when he was cooking. He passed away when I was seven. I wasn't interested in the food because I was too young, but I just remember how fascinated I was watching him in the kitchen.

What inspires you?

Small things from my daily life. Like when I'm having tea, I'll suddenly think what would it be like to make consommé with tea.

I like red wine and bonito, blue cheese and red wine; they all go together well, so this will be a new dish. Bonito is in season right now. I made blue cheese powder, grilled the bonito, and added some walnuts and raisins.

I change my dishes depending on the season. I change little by little over time. I really can't stand cooking the same dishes all the time. I can't always have the same things.

Why a seafood-only restaurant?

I wanted to do something that no one was doing. And I love fish; I'm good at cooking fish.

What motivates you?

Other chefs really, like Hiroyasu Kawate [page 15]. Also Shuzo Kishida [page 93], who I used to work for, motivate me. I feel that if I focus on fish, perhaps I can become better than they are one day. I am eager to improve and advance in my career. I can see what I am going to become, and that my food is getting better and better.

What is your earliest food memory?

I loved *karaage* [fried chicken], especially from my grandfather. I can still remember the taste of it. I was in Yokohama, about four or five years old. My grandfather really liked to drink, so my family often went to a favorite *izakaya* to eat. The *karaage* was from this *izakaya*. I would always sit next to my grandfather, and he would share his *karaage* with me.

What was one of your most valuable experiences living in Marseille?

I wanted to work in a three-Michelin-starred restaurant in France. I wrote to them all—forty of them—and Le Petit Nice replied. Some others did, too, but I accepted the first one that replied. I stayed for one year. Le Petit Nice focused on the love of fish. Working at this restaurant helped me decide that I wanted to focus on seafood when I came back to Japan.

For you, what does it mean to be Japanese?

Our attention to detail. Everything we create is so detailed, and I am proud of this.

If you could share a meal with anyone, who would it be?

Ichiro, who now plays for the Miami Marlins.

Kazutoshi Sakurai, the lead vocalist of Mr. Children, a Japanese rock band.

Yutaka Take, a jockey.

What do you like to eat on your day off?

Sushi.

What is your favorite word?

Evolution. I strive to become better and change a bit every day.

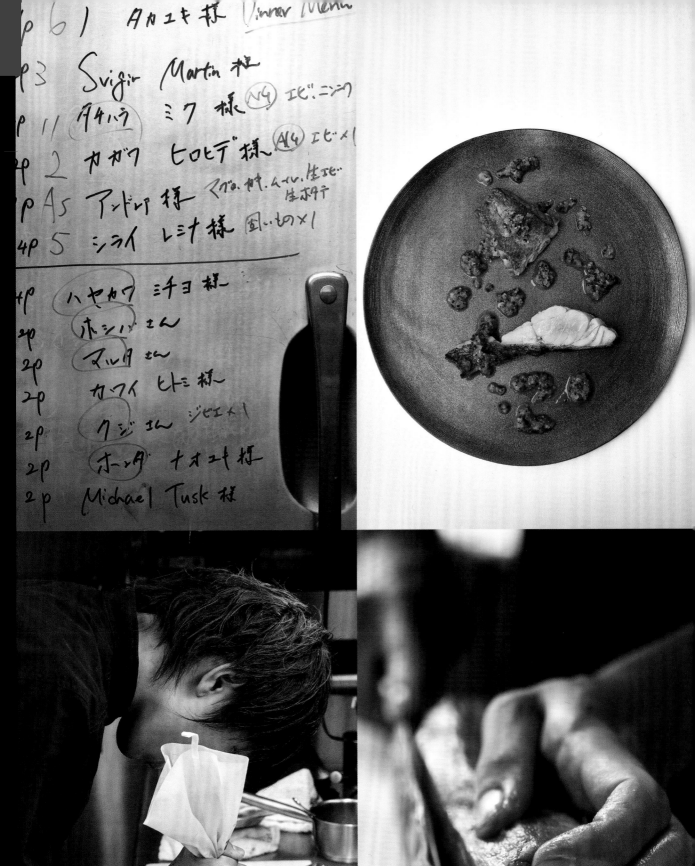

BISQUE BALLS

When I was thinking about creating a bite-size Japanese-style dish, I came up with the idea of making takoyaki *(a ball-shaped snack made of wheat flour, usually stuffed with octopus), which I always enjoy. I thought it would be interesting for the dish to look like Japanese* takoyaki, *but taste like French lobster bisque.*

FISH STOCK

2 pounds red sea bream or red snapper bones and heads

2 tablespoons sea salt

2 quarts plus 8½ cups water

LOBSTER BISQUE

8 lobster heads (see Note)

3 tablespoons olive oil, plus more for sautéing

1 onion, cut into ¾-inch cubes

1 carrot, peeled and cut into ¾-inch cubes

1 celery stalk, cut into ¾-inch cubes

1 shallot, cut into ¾-inch cubes

3 cloves garlic, minced

2 tablespoons tomato paste

1 cup white wine

2 tablespoons Cognac

Sea salt

BISQUE BALLS

¼ cup plus 1 tablespoon cake flour

2 tablespoons grated Japanese yam

1 teaspoon baking powder

½ beaten egg

1 teaspoon white soy sauce

½ teaspoon sea salt

Olive oil, for cooking

3 tablespoons chopped fresh flat-leaf parsley

SERVES 4 TO 6

To make the fish stock, place the fish bones and heads in a large bowl, sprinkle with the salt, and let sit for 10 minutes.

To remove the fishy odor of the bones, bring 2 quarts of the water to a boil. Pour the water over the fish bones and heads and drain.

Place the fish bones and heads and the 8½ cups water into a large stockpot and bring to a boil over medium heat. When the water just starts to boil, turn the heat to low and skim off any scum. Cook for 30 minutes. Strain the stock through a fine-mesh sieve into a bowl, discard the solids, and set aside.

To make the bisque, remove lobster meat from the shells. Be sure to remove the sand sac. Finely chop the little bit of lobster meat you have, including from the legs.

In a Dutch oven, pour just enough olive oil to coat the bottom of the pan and heat over medium heat. Add the lobster meat and sauté for 10 minutes, until most of the juices have cooked off. Add the

onion, carrot, celery, shallot, garlic, tomato paste, and remaining 3 tablespoons olive oil and cook for about 3 minutes more, until the vegetables visibly soften and become translucent. Add the white wine and Cognac and simmer until most of the liquid has evaporated. Add 5 cups of the fish stock and simmer for 20 minutes more, until reduced by half. Strain the bisque through a fine-mesh sieve and discard the solids.

Return the bisque to a clean pot, bring to a simmer, and cook until it has been reduced to 1 cup, 10 to 20 minutes. Season with sea salt to taste. Let cool to room temperature and set aside.

To make the bisque balls, combine the lobster bisque, cake flour, yam, baking powder, egg, soy sauce, and salt in a bowl and stir together with a spoon. Cover the batter and refrigerate overnight.

The next day, transfer the batter to a liquid measuring cup. Coat a *takoyaki* pan with olive oil and warm the pan over medium heat. Working in batches, pour about 1 tablespoon batter into each hole in the pan to fill to about three-fourths full. Cook until the bottoms are golden brown, 2 to 3 minutes. Turn them with a metal skewer and cook until the other sides are golden brown, about 2 minutes more. Transfer the balls to a bowl by removing them from the pan with a skewer. Keep warm while you cook the remaining balls, oiling the pan again if needed.

Place 3 to 5 balls on each plate and sprinkle chopped parsley on top. Serve immediately.

NOTE: A *takoyaki* pan is required for this recipe. You will need to start one day ahead to make the stock and bisque and then let the batter sit overnight. In Japan, lobster heads refer to the front section of the lobster that includes the legs, but not the claw. If you can't get those, use the meat from four lobster tails, chopped, instead.

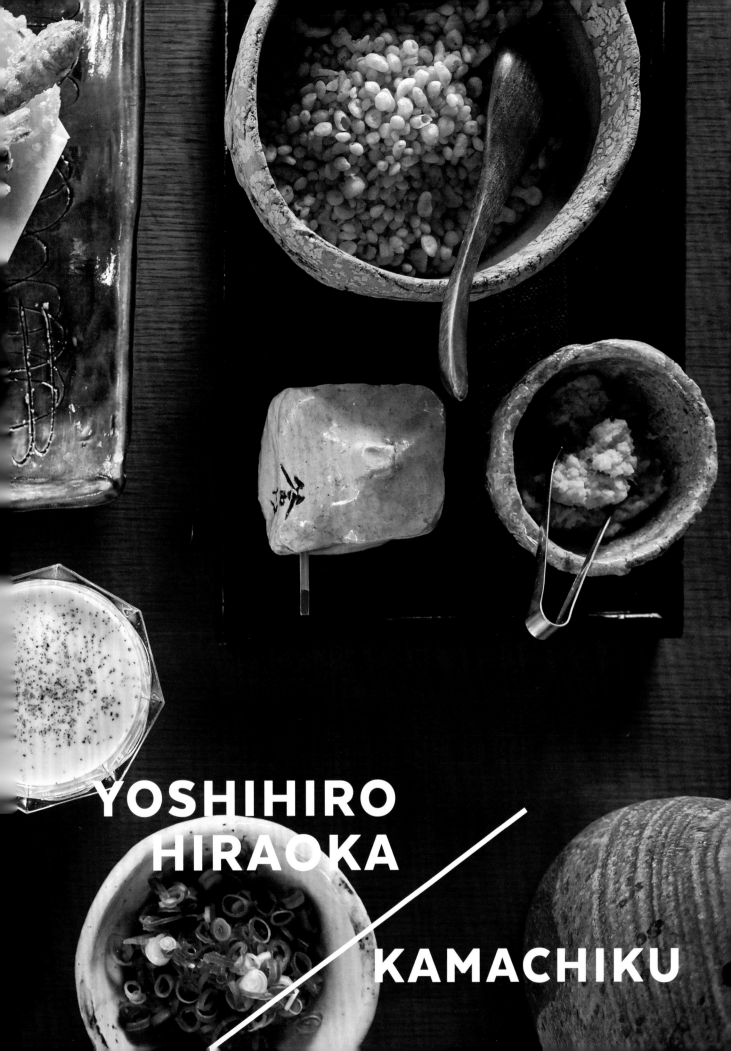

YOSHIHIRO
HIRAOKA

KAMACHIKU

LEGACY

DEVOTION

In a one-hundred-year-old building on a tranquil street corner in Nezu, a restaurant anchors an imposing dark wood, metal, and brick building reconfigured and reimagined by famed architect Kengo Kuma. As I stand in its lush central garden looking at a quiet koi-filled pond, I notice the reflections of the garden on the glass facade create the illusion that diners at a communal table inside are eating outside, surrounded by nature. Up a few stairs inside a stocky brick tower, a remnant of the private home this used to be, a dark and traditional space is brought alive by the sound of otherwise quiet diners reverently slurping noodles.

Here at Kamachiku, in the gentle hands of chef-owner Yoshihiro Hiraoka, diners learn just how exquisite udon noodles can be. Hiraoka's udon are of a consistency, flavor, and quality not often experienced outside Japan, and are the centerpiece of a myriad of condiments and small dishes stunning for their sheer variety alone. *Tamago* (Japanese-style omelet), luxurious handmade sesame tofu, crunchy radish salad, and stuffed fish cake are just a few of the dishes that I savored on my first visit. The condiments include fresh grated ginger (my favorite) and *agedama*, the crunchy little bits of fried tempura batter. The long udon noodles are served just two ways: cold (*zaru* udon) or hot (*kamaage* udon) with dashi stock.

Chef Hiraoka emerges from his steamy kitchen, perspiring with a towel draped around his neck. He greets me with a deep bow, telling me how honored he is that I have returned to his restaurant to meet with him. He is soft-spoken—sweet and deferential—with a broad boyish face and wavy, reddish hair. Now thirty-six, he grew up in his father's udon shop, also called Kamachiku, in Osaka. And though he was not planning to follow in his father's footsteps, he jumped at the chance to move to Tokyo to open a restaurant of his own in a building designed by Kengo Kuma. Initially, Hiraoka wanted to make a good living in order to buy his dream sports car. He dedicated himself to the pursuit of perfect udon, and along the way, he literally fell in love with his work. The fact that customers wait in line for his udon—and there is always a long line—is humbling to Hiraoka. It is his greatest hope that he has made his cherished grandfather and father proud, and that one day he can pass Kamachiku on to one of his sons.

INTERVIEW

Why do you cook?

I wanted to be a systems engineer, and I almost got a job offer. I was never really interested in food but because my dad's restaurant was very famous, I was always exposed to it. My dad didn't want me to be a chef. He wanted me to be a businessman. Being a chef is tough. But once I started learning, I got really into it and all I wanted was to be a chef. My dad is a *shokunin* [master artisan]. My mom managed my dad's restaurant. I was inspired by my parents and their work at the restaurant, and how they made something great together. I want to combine the best aspects from my dad and my mom; it would be great to adapt traits from both of them to become the perfect man.

How do you think your generation differs from those that came before you?

The men of my dad's generation had to do a lot on their own. They concentrated on one type of food, and it was harder to get information. I think my father's generation was more inquisitive. I opened my restaurant with the same name, and I must do well by my dad and make it bigger and better. I don't want to compromise anything; I want to make my father proud. Today, so many chefs learn from others. We don't study by ourselves but have many more influences.

For you, what does it mean to be Japanese?

Nihon ryori [Japanese cuisine] and the counter style. Also the sushi *shokunin* [master artisan] and their highly detailed style of cooking are all connected to the distinct form of Japanese hospitality for me.

Who do you admire in the food world?

I'm so impressed by sushi masters. Sometimes I look at the customers through the window and I change the udon width and texture and details based on what my customers convey to me. That's what sushi masters do.

If you could share a meal with anyone, who would it be?

Ichiro, the baseball player for the Miami Marlins; he's so stoic and cool and very smart.

Ojiichan, my mother's father. I want to tell him that I have opened this restaurant and that it's successful.

My mother and father. My mom came from a family of dried-bonito store owners. My dad came from a family of sake brewers. It was a perfect match.

Do you have a favorite word?

Kamachiku. A *kama* is a huge cauldron and *chiku* is a reference to the characters that make up my father's name. I think this name has spirit!

KAMAAGE UDON

My father made this udon when I was growing up. It has always been a part of my life, and I am proud to be able to make it for my customers in Tokyo. Kamaage udon are noodles served in a bowl of hot water to keep them warm and fresh, next to a bowl of hot dashi stock for dipping along with several toppings. Following tradition, you knead the dough for the udon noodles with your feet.

NOODLES

1 cup bottled or soft water

4 teaspoons salt

¾ cup plus 1 tablespoon cake flour

DASHI STOCK

2 strips dried kombu (seaweed), each approximately 12 by 2 inches

2 quarts room-temperature bottled or soft water

1 tablespoon dried mackerel flakes

2½ tablespoons dried bonito flakes

¾ cup regular soy sauce

4 tablespoons light soy sauce

4 teaspoons nikiri sake

4 tablespoons sugar

TOPPINGS

Thinly sliced green onion

Grated fresh ginger

Shichimi togarashi (five-spice powder)

Corn starch, for dusting

SERVES 4

To make the noodles, Day 1: Stir together the water and salt in a glass bowl and let sit at room temperature overnight. (At this point, start making the dashi stock, too.)

Day 2: Put the flour in another bowl. Slowly drizzle the salted water, little by little, into the flour, mixing constantly by hand. Keep doing this until all of the water is added, and knead with your hands until the texture becomes soft and elastic, 10 to 15 minutes. The dough will look like a silky ball at this point, as if you are baking bread.

Remove the dough from the bowl and put in a large ziplock bag. Seal, then place inside another ziplock bag, and place a few sheets of plastic wrap on the floor. Place the wrapped dough on the floor and, without shoes, step on the dough, up and down, for about 3 minutes. Let the dough rest for 30 minutes. Then repeat step-kneading and rest the dough two more times, until all of the air is removed from the dough. Refrigerate the wrapped dough and let rest at least overnight and up to 3 days.

To make the dashi stock, Day 1: Cut the kombu strips into small pieces about 2 inches wide and combine with the water in a large pot. Let rest overnight.

Day 2: Place the stock over medium heat. Just before the water starts to boil, remove the kombu with a spider strainer or small fine-mesh sieve. Skim off any scum once the water starts boiling, then add the dried mackerel and boil for 10 minutes. Skim off any scum again, then add the dried bonito and turn the heat to low and simmer for 5 minutes. Remove from the heat, cover the pot, and let steam for 5 minutes more.

Strain the dashi through a cheesecloth-lined fine-mesh sieve set over another pot. Add the regular soy sauce, light soy sauce, sake, and sugar. Place the pot over high heat and remove from the heat just before the stock starts to boil once again. Cover and let steam for 5 minutes more. Transfer to a nonreactive bowl, let the stock cool to room temperature, then place in the refrigerator to rest overnight.

Day 3: Heat the dashi stock over low heat until hot. Keep warm. Place the toppings in bowls to serve at the table.

Bring a large pot of water, such as a pasta pot, to a boil over high heat.

On a wood surface dusted with corn starch, roll the dough out with a wooden rolling pin until it is ⅛ inch thick. Cut the dough into strips that are ⅛ to ¼ inch wide and 12 inches long.

Add all of the noodles to the boiling water and cook for 8 minutes, until a little bit softer than al dente. Be careful that the water doesn't overboil because of the starch in the dough. Remove the noodles from the water with a hand colander or prepare another empty pot with a strainer on top of it and pour in the cooked noodles, retaining the cooking liquid.

Place the noodles in deep individual soup or noodle bowls with tongs. Pour just enough of the hot cooking water over the udon to make the noodles float. In four smaller bowls, such as rice bowls, pour the hot dashi stock for dipping.

Serve immediately, having diners use chopsticks to lift each mouthful of noodles out of the hot water and into the dashi stock. Season with the green onions, ginger, and shichimi togarashi to taste.

NOTE: You need to start this recipe three days before serving it, and note that both the noodles and stock require preparation two days in advance. Yoshihiro Hiraoka prefers using soft water to make the noodles and dashi stock. If that's not what flows through your tap, he recommends using bottled water instead. Instead of making your own stock, you can also use instant dashi in powder or teabag form. *Nikiri* sake, a lower-alcohol version of sake, is available at Japanese specialty grocers.

SHINYA
OTSUCHIHASHI

CRAFTALE

FLARE

NOSTALGIA

Craftale is in the lush Nakameguro neighborhood along the canal-like Meguro river. It is up on the second floor, with a view of the water and the cherry trees. Shinya Otsuchihashi is thirty-two, and has an exceptional curiosity for ingredients; before we begin our interview, he completely dissects an okra flower. With a sense of wonder and tweezers, he reveals its yellow-and-purple paperlike petals, explaining its components to me like a botanist.

We sit down at a wooden table in Craftale's placid, spare dining area, which recalls Nordic minimalism. The gray, beige, and white space has an industrial look, with unfinished building materials integrated into the design. Most of the dining room faces a single large rectangular window that looks out onto the canal; the L-shaped open kitchen sits at the entrance.

Otsuchihashi is a young man transformed by his time living and cooking abroad in France, but not by the country alone. He stresses the life-changing, revelatory excitement he experienced interacting with young chefs from the world over, all of whom traveled to France to work and gain experience just as he did. His family's devotion and love are also a source of creativity and motivation. A sense of honor and maturity beyond his years is strong within him; he wishes to be successful so that he can reflect well on all those who have worked with him, supported him, and believed in him.

Eating at Craftale means enjoying a succession of small dishes that are well thought out and adventurous in terms of color, texture, and provenance. One of the dishes I recently enjoyed is Galician octopus. I happened to share it with a Galician friend, and we both agreed that Otsuchihashi succeeded in transporting us to Spain. But Otsuchihashi's penchant for conveying a sense of place is not limited to one country. He will often use unconventional materials in lieu of traditional ceramic plates, like a wooden block, a crystal cylindrical platform, or a square stone slate. Eclectic breadlike creations are made specifically for main dishes and presented as accompaniments, something he calls bread pairings. For example, an empanada with a twist is served with the octopus, or a flaky escargot-swirled bread accompanies his escargot. His presentation can be arresting and innovative, something that makes eating here both fun and noteworthy. It seems that Michelin has discovered Otsuchihashi and agrees with me; they have awarded him his first star.

INTERVIEW

Why do you cook?

I cook because I am very much a gourmand. I eat all the time. I always wanted to eat the best food in the world, and then just decided to make it myself. It evolved into preparing food for others. I wanted to work in a restaurant to express my understanding of ingredients and share my philosophy on the plate. I like to communicate the scenery from where the ingredients came from, the environment and origins of the food. This is why my dishes change with the seasons. I think if customers eat what I create, they will recall these things, no matter where they are from.

How did living in France affect you?

In Japan, we express ideas and emotions indirectly. This is because of the religion and culture. We learn in elementary school and high school to be a bit shy and are tentative about being rejected by others. I don't think this is wrong; this way of expression is communal. Before I went to France, my way of thinking was rigid, and then when I was there, my way of thinking changed. There was more freedom to express myself more easily. It was the best experience of my life. In the kitchen each month in France, there were three people from all over the world who came to work for one month. Just two of us had fixed positions, everyone else changed. I learned a lot from these international visitors.

What motivates you?

I do what I do for my family and for myself. The people I work with and my immediate family are important to me. They are actually all one big extended family.

What is your earliest food memory?

My bento box that my mom would make when I went to school in Kagoshima. It wasn't tasty, but I remember it well. She always gave me the same thing, with little things on the side. There was always *tamago* [Japanese-style omelet], small tomatoes, vegetables, fish, and a lot of rice. The lunch box wasn't big, but my mother stuffed it with all these things, and the tomato was always crushed on top of the rice. I realize now, with a sense of nostalgia, that my mom was considering the balance of the food— egg, fish, vegetable, rice.

Tell me about the name Craftale.

It comes from Craft and Tale. Craft is the making of something, creating a story. Tale is a story, the menu itself.

For you, what does it mean to be Japanese?

People caring about others, manners. Rice. I love Japanese rice. When I was in France, I wanted to eat steamed white rice. I really wanted it. I lost weight in Paris and gained it back here in Japan.

What do you like most about Tokyo?

It's a small world here. We have everything, and it's really intense. It's a great fusion of nature and city.

Do you have a favorite word?

I have a favorite phrase: Live true to yourself.

What is one of your favorite films?

Miyazaki's *Castle in the Sky*. There's a lot of food and food references in the film. When I was little and I saw this film, there were many things I wanted to eat.

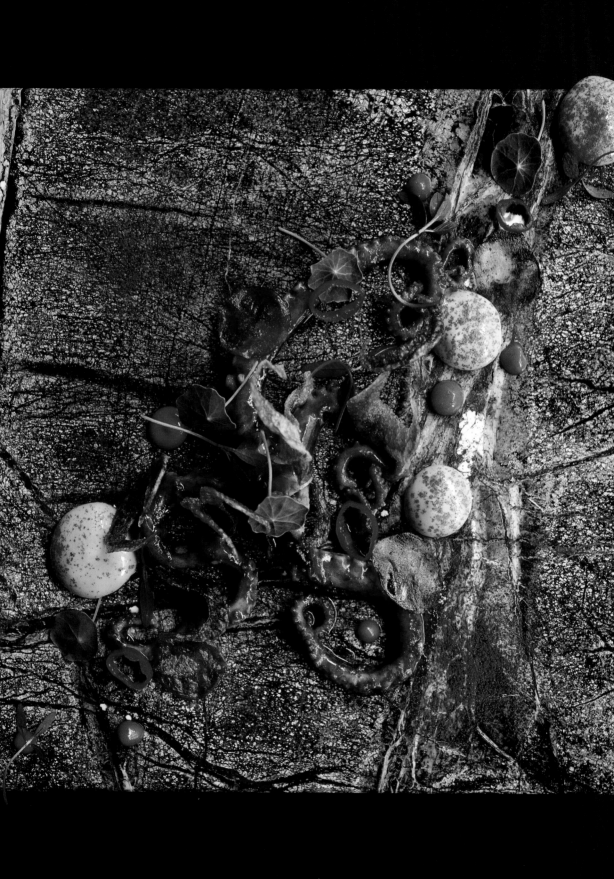

GALICIAN-STYLE OCTOPUS WITH POTATO CHIPS

Since childhood, I have always thought about food. I wanted to create a summer dish with octopus, a popular and inexpensive ingredient that can be used to create interesting and modern presentations. I use an octopus called tenagadako *(long-armed octopus). It has a soft texture and vibrant and lively visual appeal when cooked. To me, it looks as if it is dancing flamenco on the plate! To further convey the passion and vibrancy of flamenco, I incorporate red ingredients, too, like red bell pepper and paprika.*

POTATO CHIPS

1 purple or yellow potato

1 pink or yellow potato

¼ cup olive oil

OCTOPUS CONFIT

1 clove garlic, peeled and chopped

2 rosemary sprigs

4 thyme sprigs

1¼ cups olive oil

2 small octopi, about ½ pound each

ANCHOVY SAUCE

3 eggs

3½ tablespoons olive oil

2-ounce tin of anchovies in olive oil, drained, skinned, and deboned

2 teaspoons sweet paprika

RED PEPPER SAUCE

5 red bell peppers

½ cup olive oil

Salt

15 nasturtium leaves

15 fresh basil leaves

Paprika, for garnish

SERVES 5

To make the potato chips, preheat the oven to 275°F.

Cut the potatoes with a mandoline into 1/16-inch-thick slices. Put the potatoes onto a baking sheet in one layer. Brush the olive oil on top to cover. Bake for about 90 minutes, until dry and transparent.

Lower the oven temperature to 175°F.

To make the octopus confit, sauté the garlic, rosemary, and thyme in the olive oil in small sauté pan over low heat for 2 minutes, just to bring out the perfume of the herbs. Transfer the oil and herbs to a 3-quart saucepan.

Remove the heads from the octopi by holding the whole octopus, by the tentacles, and pulling. Then clean out the heads. Cut the tentacles into sections with three tentacles each. Put the tentacles and heads in the seasoned olive oil and cook in the oven for 3 hours until a deep, almost reddish brown. Keep warm.

To make the anchovy sauce, bring a small pot of water to a rolling boil and also prepare an ice bath. Cook the eggs in the boiling water for 5 minutes. Drain, place the eggs in the ice bath for 5 minutes, and then peel.

Combine the eggs, olive oil, anchovies, and paprika in a blender and puree until smooth. Strain through a fine-mesh chinois. Discard any solids.

To make the red pepper sauce, remove the bell pepper skins with a peeler, then remove the seeds. Cut the peppers lengthwise into three or four pieces.

Heat the olive oil in small sauté pan over medium heat. Add the peppers and sauté for 20 minutes, until very wilted and soft. Pour the peppers into a blender with a pinch of salt and puree until smooth. Strain with a fine-mesh sieve and discard the solids.

Put the anchovy sauce and red pepper sauce each into plastic squeeze bottles. Remove the octopus confit from the pan with tongs. Place on some paper towels to remove most of the oil. Cut the heads into three pieces.

For each serving, place three tentacles and a piece of the head on a plate. Squeeze a small dot of anchovy sauce and a small dot of red pepper sauce close to the octopus. Lean the potato chips against the octopus. Scatter three nasturtium and three basil leaves over the dish. Sprinkle the paprika over three points around the octopus. Serve immediately.

MAKOTO
KONNO

ORGAN

NECESSITY

INDEPENDENCE

In the dining room at Organ, a turntable plays John Coltrane's *Live at the Village Vanguard*, the record sleeve propped up on display. Books line a shelf right beneath the pass, reading material for those who care to indulge. These say a lot about Makoto Konno, together with the eclectic collections of chairs and tables, the large refrigerator filled exclusively with natural wines, and the enticing aromas coming from the galley kitchen.

Konno's hair is pulled back into an attractive low ponytail. His loose posture and bearing are not typically Japanese; he does not bow, and he sits across from me with an arm propped up on one chair, legs crossed. This observation makes sense when I discover that Konno lived in Southern California for ten years. His experience living abroad informed much of what interests him and helped to develop his aesthetic and beliefs about food and food culture.

Konno identifies strongly with the saying, "Necessity is the mother of invention"; he did not grow up with means, but often faced choices in life based on need. He is not impressed by wealth or corporate influence and does not feel that dining should be a rarefied experience only available to those who can afford it. The chairs I notice upon entering Organ are meaningful to Konno, symbolizing creativity, art, individuality, independence, and a disregard for corporate sameness. When I ask why these traits are important to him, he answers with a smile, "Because I am a rocker." He is a rocker who loves film; a rocker who loves natural wines and food; a rocker who values openness and the creative process.

Konno's pioneering status supporting natural wines in Japan also illustrates his conviction and unconventional status. Natural wines are the product of grapes left alone to go through their own fermentation process without chemicals of any kind. He serves these products exclusively from the small, modest vineyards that make them, often not turning a profit.

Although his food at Organ is hearty, based on the French bistro tradition, his dishes also incorporate ideas and elements from other cultures that Konno absorbed while living in California. There is crab with avocado, apple, celery root, and lemongrass mayonnaise; or roasted lamb with yuzu *harissa*.

Some of the most compelling chefs are those who are down-to-earth, cooking to express an idea larger than themselves. At Organ, Konno has created a place where life is unhurried—where guests can savor good food, pure natural wine, and powerful music. Here, individual expression has a home; sameness is nowhere in sight.

INTERVIEW

What was it like for you when you arrived in Los Angeles?

It was my first time outside Japan. I didn't know how long we would stay. I didn't speak English or have a driver's license. The first thing I did was buy a bicycle. I wanted to see the ocean, so I went on my bicycle without realizing how far it was. There was a hill in a nearby town, and I saw the ocean from the top of it. So I knew I was in California! I was so tired. I couldn't go all the way to the ocean. In Los Angeles, I learned independence. I saw that in the cafés people wanted to express themselves. There was a subculture of creativity. People who create very new things are often under pressure, because they don't have money. Need often creates creativity. I didn't see this in Japan, and I loved it.

What is the origin of the names Organ and Uguisu, your wine bar?

Organ is literally the name of the large musical instrument. *Uguisu* is a bird, the Japanese bush warbler.

What is your cooking style?

It's based on French, but I add different elements and ideas and things I tasted at the restaurants in Los Angeles—Mexican, Korean, Southeast Asian, African.

In the United States, what did it mean for you to be Japanese?

It meant I was an immigrant. My parents could have stayed in the United States indefinitely, but they decided to return to Japan. It felt limiting to me to be in the United States—I had a business visa and did not enjoy the same benefits as a citizen. I was existing somewhere between being an immigrant and a foreigner. America gave me a lot of new and positive things, though. People there are more direct and more straightforward with goals and what they do or how they think. The Japanese way is more indirect.

And now that you have returned to Japan?

I feel a little different than a typical Japanese because of the long time I lived abroad. I am proud of my experience in the United States. I am more decisive and more open. I have been influenced by many cultures.

What is your earliest food memory?

Oyako-donburi. We called it mother and son, the chicken and egg. My father used to take me fishing, and we would stop at a Japanese family restaurant to have it.

If you could share a meal with anyone, who would it be?

Wes Anderson. I love his movies as much as I love Jim Jarmusch movies.

Matthew Barney, an American artist.

Claude Courtois, a winemaker in the Loire Valley.

Tell me about your love of natural wines.

Fourteen years ago, when I started my wine bar, Uguisu, there were no words or classification for natural wines. I started collecting these cloudy wines and started studying them. I liked that each wine was different, just as I like to be on the opposite side of big money, big corporations. After you open the bottle, the taste changes.

Natural wine is different from organic wine. It is also organic, but the production is actually a lot more strict, with no chemicals in the production from beginning to end. It is also unfiltered.

What is your favorite word?

It's actually a saying: "Better today than yesterday. Better tomorrow than today."

What are your favorite films?

Paris, Texas, directed by Wim Wenders; *Stranger Than Paradise* and *Dead Man*, directed by Jim Jarmusch; and *City of God*, directed by Fernando Meirelles.

SALTED AGED PORK BELLY WITH LENTILS AND POACHED EGG

I am constantly searching for new ideas from global cuisines for my own creations, but always try to keep some traditional French dishes on my menu. When I ask myself what I want to serve my customers, the answer is simply something that tastes good. This is the French petit salé aux lentilles. *I top it with a poached egg.*

PORK BELLY

Salt

2 pounds pork belly
(preferably skin-on)

2½ quarts water

½ cup white wine

1 onion, cut into 1-inch-thick
slices

1 carrot, peeled and cut into
1-inch-thick slices

1 celery stalk, cut into
1-inch-thick slices

1 clove garlic, peeled and halved

2 bay leaves

2 thyme sprigs

1 rosemary sprig

3 star anise

2 cloves

1 tablespoon Dijon mustard

3 tablespoons panko
bread crumbs

LENTILS

1 tablespoon olive oil

⅓ cup chopped onion

⅓ cup chopped carrot

⅓ cup chopped celery

2½ cups green lentils,
thoroughly washed

3 ounces bacon, cooked
and chopped

1 tablespoon tomato paste

1½ teaspoons coriander seeds

1 teaspoon cumin seeds

2 thyme sprigs

4 cups water

1 tablespoon white wine vinegar

1 egg

Chopped fresh flat-leaf parsley,
for garnish

SERVES 4

To make the pork belly, rub approximately 2 tablespoons salt all over the pork belly, cover with paper towels, and dry-age in the refrigerator for 4 to 7 days.

In a large Dutch oven, combine the pork belly, water, wine, onion, carrot, celery, garlic, bay leaves, thyme, rosemary, star anise, and cloves. Bring to a boil over high heat, then cover, lower the heat, and simmer for 2 hours, until tender. Remove the pork belly from the cooking liquid and slice ½ inch thick. Reserve the remaining cooking liquid.

To make the lentils, warm the olive oil a Dutch oven over low heat. Add the onion, carrot, and celery and sauté for 10 minutes, until the mixture softens and the onion is translucent. Add the lentils and sauté for 2 to 3 minutes, until coated with oil. Stir in the bacon. Add 1½ quarts of the reserved pork belly cooking liquid and bring to a boil. Lower the heat, add the tomato paste, coriander, cumin, and thyme and simmer for 30 minutes, until the lentils soften.

To finish the pork belly, preheat the oven to 425°F. Spread the pork belly slices out in single layer in a baking dish. Slather the pork belly with the mustard and sprinkle with the panko. Bake for 5 minutes, until the bread crumbs brown.

While the pork is cooking, poach the egg. Bring the water to a boil in a small saucepan over high heat. Add the vinegar and turn off the heat. While circulating the water with a spoon, crack the egg into the water and turn the heat back on to low. Cook for 1½ minutes without stirring.

Spoon the lentils onto a serving platter and place the pork belly on top. Sprinkle with parsley, place the poached egg on top, and break the yolk so it flows nicely over the entire dish. Serve immediately.

NOTE: You need to start this recipe four to seven days in advance.

TAKAO ISHIYAMA

SUSHIYA

QUIET

DISCIPLINE

Japanese culture values silence in interactions with others. *Chinmoku* (silence) is considered an essential form of communication; it's not just the lack of words or random pauses within a conversation but the deliberate choice to convey a thought or idea by being quiet. Often *chinmoku* is more important and powerful than what words can convey. Understanding the power of silence is integral to understanding others' intentions and Japan itself.

Takao Ishiyama is quiet.

The first time I meet Ishiyama at Sushiya, his bijou restaurant on a narrow Ginza side alleyway, he is not easy to read nor prone to expressions of emotion. He has a serious bearing and the demeanor of someone way beyond his years. He is only thirty-two, quite young to be so admired as a sushi master. When he speaks, he does so in a hesitating, hushed voice. He exudes an almost military-like aura: even, controlled, and undemonstrative.

Ishiyama agrees to meet me at a café in Yoyogi weeks later. He is almost unrecognizable when he enters. Gone is the classic appearance of a sushi chef; in its place is a young guy wearing shorts, a Champion T-shirt, and Michael Jordan sneakers. He looks at least ten years younger. He still has the same quiet, calm, measured voice when we begin to chat, but is a lot more animated today, smiling frequently. I mention that he seems different outside his restaurant, which he acknowledges as true. Working with sushi and leading a staff where he is considered the master imparts a different bearing. Not only a different posture and way of carrying himself, but a different state of mind. Ishiyama is always rather quiet though, he says, no matter where he is.

When having dinner at Sushiya, in a classically charming setting, perhaps it is difficult to imagine that his idol is Michael Jordan. Ishiyama is a skilled basketball player, but is now concerned about hurting his hands. He did not learn to be a sushi chef in culinary school, but rather by apprenticing, which is more common. He previously trained at both the respected Sushi Kanesaka and the revered three-Michelin-starred Sushi Saito. He says his strong point is his *nigiri*, and his loyal following supports this assertion.

As we share tea and chat, there are consistent gaps of silence and reflection. When I ask if he has a favorite word that best reflects who he is, without hesitation he says "peace."

You are very young; how is it that you already have your own *sushi-ya*?

I trained at the main branch of Kanesaka in Ginza and practiced a lot by watching the senior chef. It was decided that another place would be opened in Ginza, which was originally Sushi Iwa. Kanesaka made me head chef here. I was twenty-eight, the youngest head sushi chef in Ginza, maybe Tokyo.

You worked for Takashi Saito, the famed three-star Michelin chef. What did you learn from him?

I supported him; there were only two of us. I had to do the preparation of rice with the vinegar, as well as filleting the fish. During service, I grilled the fish, and served the sake and tea. Any of the things Saito didn't do.

What is so appealing to you about sushi?

First of all, it's tasty. Second, it's beautiful. I do know about the history, which is interesting. Mine is Edomae or Edo-style. I didn't choose this style; it's what I learned from the beginning.

What is the most essential part of making excellent sushi?

The action itself of making the sushi, the balance between the rice, vinegar, and fish. How the rice is cooked and for how long, the cutting of the fish to make one piece of sushi, and the quantity of the *shari* from the *ohitsu* [wood container]. I use *sake kasu* [sake lees] vinegar, not rice vinegar.

What is your earliest food memory?

My mother's gyoza.

For you, what does it mean to be Japanese?

I've never thought about it before. For me, perhaps it is deep love for sushi and the way I work.

What do you do in your free time?

Basketball. I used to play with a team, but since I work, I can't play. I also protect my hands and fingers. Some days I go just to play a bit.

What do you like to eat on your day off?

Sushi!

MACKEREL BOUZUSHI (PRESSED SUSHI)

This recipe is from the Kansai area, where Kyoto and Osaka are. It wasn't at all common in Tokyo when I first started making this. I think it looks very beautiful, and the way the fish and rice are compressed together makes it taste particularly good.

MACKEREL

1 whole chub mackerel (masaba), 15 to 16 inches long and about 1 pound (ask your fishmonger to clean, debone, and fillet)

Salt

17 ounces rice vinegar, chilled

KOMBU

4 sheets dried kombu (seaweed), each about 10 by 6 inches

2 cups mirin

2 cups rice vinegar

¼ cup granulated sugar

2 cups Japanese short-grain rice

2 tablespoons rice vinegar

2 teaspoons salt

Pinch of sugar (optional)

Toasted sesame seeds

16 to 20 pieces pickled ginger

4 fresh shiso leaves, each sliced into 3 pieces

MAKES 4 ROLLS

To make the mackerel, rub the fillets all over with salt until covered in a thin layer and let sit at room temperature for 2 hours. Wash off the salt and dry with paper towels. Put the mackerel in a baking dish and cover with the vinegar. Let soak at room temperature for 20 minutes. Cover and refrigerate overnight.

To make the kombu, place the pieces in a large stockpot wide enough to fit them. Add the mirin, vinegar, and sugar and cook over low heat until the kombu softens, about 1 hour, covered.

Remove the pot from the heat. Leave the kombu in the pot until it cools to room temperature. Cover and refrigerate overnight.

The next day, remove the mackerel from the vinegar and place on a cutting board. Remove any remaining bones with tweezers and remove the skin. Place the fillets skin side down on the cutting board. Cut the fillets lengthwise into two pieces. Score the skin side of each of the pieces ¼ inch deep.

Cook the rice.

While the rice cooks, whisk together the rice vinegar and salt in a small bowl. Whisk in the sugar, if you desire.

Transfer the cooked rice to a bowl, and while it's still hot, use a rice paddle to mix it with the seasoned vinegar. Let cool to room temperature.

To assemble a roll, pat the kombu pieces dry. Place a sheet of plastic wrap on a sushi mat. Place one piece of kombu on the plastic wrap, followed by one piece of mackerel. Spread a layer of room-temperature rice with a rice paddle. Sprinkle with sesame seeds, four or five pieces of pickled ginger, and slices of shiso leaf. Roll and shape the roll with the mat. Cut into ½- to ¾-inch slices. Repeat with the remaining ingredients and serve immediately.

NOTE: You need to prepare the mackerel and the kombu one day in advance. Chilled rice vinegar helps remove the skin from the mackerel.

KUNIATSU KONDO
/ OWAN

SWEETNESS

REMEMBRANCE

The architect Kengo Kuma is one of Japan's most noted design talents. His buildings convey a strong sense of place and Japanese identity without feeling traditional. The Nezu Museum is one of his best-known works in Tokyo, as is the Baisoin Temple in Minami Aoyama, where I first photograph Kuniatsu Kondo.

The reinterpretation of Japanese tradition I see in Kuma's buildings I observe in Owan, Kondo's warm little *izakaya* in Ikejiri-Ohashi. The whole concept of this handsome space is centered around the bowl, or *owan*. A simple collection of predominantly lacquer bowls is displayed on illuminated shelves. Every choice of cutlery or vessel is intentional and deliberate, meant to convey the warmth and nostalgia of meals from his past. Kondo named his restaurant Owan after a feeling he remembered as a child—holding a bowl in his hands during a meal.

Kondo, forty-two, is overtly kind and gracious. I don't often use the word *sweet* to describe chefs, but it applies here. His ego is not at all evident; he is humble, unaffected, and gentle.

Three design elements at Owan further reveal a lot about Kondo. First is the absence of music. The sound of water trickling and cascading in a small receptacle at the corner of the counter is the soundtrack for Owan, together with the murmur of diners' voices. I share this observation with Kondo, who smiles, gratified that I notice.

Second is the menu. It is written and beautifully painted by the artist Koji Takano. Changed monthly, it is worth a visit just to see this artwork.

Third is the position of the seats and counter in relation to where Chef Kondo is cooking. Kondo says he spent ages with the restaurant designer painstakingly calculating the appropriate height of the counter and chairs in relation to the slightly sunken kitchen so that he would always look up at his guests, rather than look down at them. Kondo tells me that this was a deliberate choice to extend hospitality and convey his respect for his customers.

Rain is falling on the hot summer evening when I visit. I sit at the corner of the counter, savoring the sounds of the cascading water both outside and inside the restaurant. There is a crackling fire before me; fish is being grilled on skewers. Steam emanates from a large wood *ohitsu* (wood container) where handmade pork *shumai* (dumplings) are being steamed. Kondo is preparing corn tempura, *kishimen* (handmade Nagoya-style flat noodles), and potato salad. One of Kondo's staff offers me a warm towel, and I wait for my *omakase* (chef's choice) dinner to begin.

INTERVIEW

Why do you cook?

My mother owns an *izakaya* in Mikawa Anjo in Aichi prefecture where I am from. I always wanted to be like my mother, who always made people happy making Japanese food. When I was eighteen, I wanted to cook French food, but I realized that my mother was a great influence on me and that I'd rather cook *yōshoku* food [Japanese-influenced Western food].

What is your earliest food memory?

The dashi in *oden* [a one-pot dish of simmered fish cake, egg, daikon, and other vegetables] made by my grandmother. Before my mother, my grandmother ran and owned the *izakaya*. The dashi was great, and I had it every day. I just really liked it. My grandparents and I lived all together, and I always went to the kitchen. I wanted to sip the dashi.

For you, what does it mean to be Japanese?

Courtesy, manners, honesty—to do everything honestly and sincerely. Often, it's much easier to be honest, so people understand this about me. I am proud to be Japanese. I haven't seen a lot of the world. I have only been once to France; I don't have time and the opportunity to go to other countries.

What do you like most about Tokyo?

There are a lot of serious people, in a good way—sometimes stubborn in a good way, like *shokunin* [master artisans]. I love this about Japan. I wanted to be a *shokunin*. Being a *shokunin* is to have a certain spirit, more than one's age.

Do you have a goal for the future?

I don't really think about goals; I'm focused on what I have now. I think more about the present. I would like to teach cooking to children; I would like them to know that it is fun. I allow children in my restaurant, unlike most restaurants in Japan. I feel this is important.

What is your favorite word?

Shojiki, which means honesty.

What is one of your favorite films?

Cinema Paradiso. I like the soundtrack, and the story. I could watch it many times. It touches me always.

OWAN POTATO SALAD

My recipes are not inspired by something or someone. I always create my dishes with my intuition. After I create a dish like my potato salad, I will continue to tweak and improve it according to my customers' reactions and input. Usually, one would expect potato salad to be one of the fastest dishes to prepare at a restaurant or izakaya, but our potato salad is different. Nothing is made in advance. We cook the entire dish from scratch when we receive the order; this way our customers always receive the freshest food, and the freshest potato salad.

MAYONNAISE

2 egg yolks

1 tablespoon rice vinegar

Pinch of salt

Pinch of pepper

½ cup vegetable oil

OWAN SPECIAL DRESSING

⅓ cup corn oil

½ cup plus ½ tablespoon rice vinegar

3 tablespoons plus 1 teaspoon extra-virgin olive oil

3 tablespoons plus 1 teaspoon light soy sauce

1 teaspoon grated garlic

POTATO SALAD

1 medium russet potato (3 to 4 ounces)

1 egg

3 snap peas

1 teaspoon karashi (hot Japanese mustard) or Dijon mustard

Pinch of salt

Pinch of pepper

1 ounce (about 1 slice) thick-sliced bacon, cooked and cubed

2 peeled and cooked shrimp, cut into bite-size pieces

SERVES 2

To make the mayonnaise, whisk together the egg yolks, ½ tablespoon of the rice vinegar, the salt, and pepper in a bowl. Gradually add the vegetable oil and whisk continuously until it begins to thicken. Whisk in the remaining ½ tablespoon rice vinegar. Taste and adjust the seasoning.

To make the dressing, whisk together all of the ingredients in a bowl.

To make the potato salad, place the potato in a steamer and cook for about 25 minutes until soft. (If you don't have a steamer, you can put the potato on the steam function in the microwave.) Peel with a knife while still hot, and cut into chunks.

While the potato cooks, bring a small saucepan of water to boil and cook the egg until firm, about 5 minutes. Let cool, then peel. Make one nice slice of the egg for garnish and chop the rest to stir into the salad.

Return the water to a boil and blanch the snap peas until crisp-tender. Rinse in cold water to cool, then chop into quarters.

In a large bowl, whisk together 1 tablespoon of the mayonnaise, 1 tablespoon of the dressing, the karashi, salt, and pepper. Add the chopped hard-boiled egg, peas, bacon, and shrimp and stir together until combined. Add the hot potatoes. With a fork or potato masher, mash together all the ingredients until well incorporated but still chunky. Garnish with the reserved slice of egg and serve immediately.

NOTE: You will have leftover mayonnaise and dressing to use in other recipes; store each, tightly sealed, in the refrigerator. You can also use store-bought mayonnaise instead. The potato should be steamed, not boiled, and still hot when you toss the salad together.

DAISUKE
TSUJI

CONVIVIO

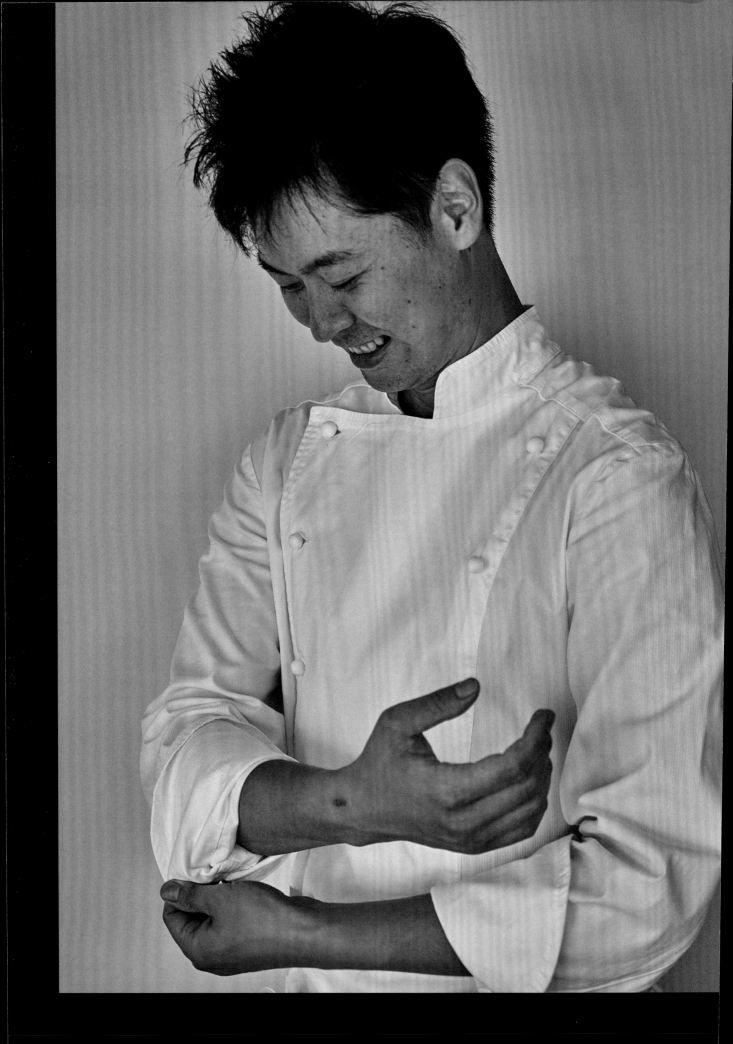

CONVICTION

DISCOVERY

Thirty-six-year-old Daisuke Tsuji greets me in Italian with an exuberant smile and a two-handed handshake. He radiates a kindness that is unmistakable; you can't help but like him. First things first, we discuss what he will cook for me. Would I like *cacio e pepe, risotto alla milanese, tonno,* or an *arista* (pork loin)? He leads me to his kitchen and I peruse the olive oils, cheeses, sea salts, and edible flowers. He removes a golden roasted pork loin from the oven, holding the pan before him like a proud father. He shares how he prepared and cooked it, before divulging more about himself; I sense that Tsuji does not speak of himself often.

Tsuji's personal story is a poignant one that conveys his self-reliance and strength of conviction. He fell in love with Italy when he was in high school, just by looking at magazines and movies. Getting there became his primary goal, taking small jobs in Tokyo in order to save enough money to buy a ticket. He had no idea about food or becoming a chef; the only desire he had was to be in Italy. He had never left Japan before.

He succeeded and arrived in Siena, at age twenty, quickly enamored by his surroundings, the art, architecture, and warmth of the people. However, three or four months after his arrival, he ran out of money. Without work, he was homeless, sleeping outside on a bench. Despite these profound challenges that would have forced many to abandon their dreams, Tsuji was resolute to stay in Italy, no matter how difficult his daily life. This tenacity kept him on his path. Doors slowly opened. An acquaintance discovered he was living outdoors and offered him shared housing, and then soon after, a job in a kitchen.

Tsuji had never trained in the food world in Tokyo or anywhere before; his eyes were opened in Italy. He experienced a personal transformation and still savors this evolution, and the impact time abroad had on his life.

His personal journey—the discovery that he loved Italy, that he loved Italian food and made it well, and that he wanted to become a chef—culminated in the opening of his own restaurant, Convivio, here in Tokyo.

As Tsuji shares his seminal stories with me, he is calm and hushed, alternatively speaking Italian and Japanese. His body language changes as he does so, further revealing the two equally integral sides of his identity, beyond what mere words can convey.

INTERVIEW

Why did you choose to go to Siena?

I went to the Italian Cultural Institute to get information and learned about Siena. It is one of the safest places in Italy and is a UNESCO World Heritage Site, with beautiful scenery and beautiful streets lined with nice houses.

How did you become a chef?

At first, I wanted to go to Italy just to live. I wanted to go there so much. I saw TV shows and magazines about Italy, Tuscany, and Milan, and it looked so beautiful to me. I worked at a gas station and at the back of a bakery packing bread to save money to be able to go to Italy. I didn't yet know that I wanted to be a chef. Then when I made it to Siena, I used up all my money so quickly that I had to live outside and sleep on a bench.

Luckily, I met a Japanese chef who wanted to return to Japan and was looking for someone to take his place. But I didn't have any experience. So I worked with him for three months and began to learn about cooking. He cooked Tuscan food. I didn't really have any idea of what it was or what I wanted to be. I just really wanted to stay in Italy. I liked the way I felt in Italy. It is not as precise as Japan is—it's more disorganized but also more spontaneous. I knew that I did not want a predictable life.

At first, I worked to survive. Living in Italy, I became stronger. I didn't panic easily. I am more expressive now. I used to be much more quiet and timid. Living in Italy changed everything about me.

What is the biggest influence on your cooking?

Antica Trattoria La Torre in Castellina, in the Chianti region. I worked there for two years. This restaurant is 125 years old. Friends of friends mentioned it to me for the first time; it is famous for its meats and traditional Tuscan cuisine. There were five grandmothers who worked there. I learned a lot from them, including Italian history. They told me so many stories.

What is your earliest food memory?

Dried daikon for *kiriboshi daikon* made by my mom, growing up in Kyoto. I remember the smell and taste. I liked how it tasted. She wasn't a great cook, but she prepared things with a lot of love.

Who do you admire in the food world?

Chef Gualtiero Marchesi, the first chef to be awarded three Michelin stars in Italy.

How do you think growing up in Japan makes you different from a native Italian chef?

I think it's difficult for Japanese to create something from scratch; instead, I think we are good at improving upon other things that others have already made.

What do you like most about Tokyo?

The polytheistic culture. We have many gods in Tokyo. This is really Japanese: we pray for the sunrise, we pray for sunset, we pray for and appreciate water. It is easy to feel all the seasons in Japan.

If you could share a meal with anyone, who would it be?

I would like to eat with members of Shinsengumi, a special police force in Kyoto organized by the military government during Japan's Bakumatsu period from 1864 to 1869.

Isami Kondo, swordsman and Edo period official.

Toshizo Hijikata, vice commander, swordsman, and military leader.

Soji Okita, captain of the first unit and revered swordsman.

What cause or charity is most important to you?

Autism. Convivio organized and did a collaboration dinner for Autism Awareness Day. I would like to do more for this cause. I would like to help people more through my food. I think it is important to connect to people and build relationships through my food.

Do you have a favorite word?

No, but I have a phrase that I like:

Domani è un'altro giorno, si vedrà.

"Tomorrow is another day, we'll see."

What is one of your favorite films?

Life Is Beautiful, I saw it on TV right before going to Italy, and it helped me to learn Italian.

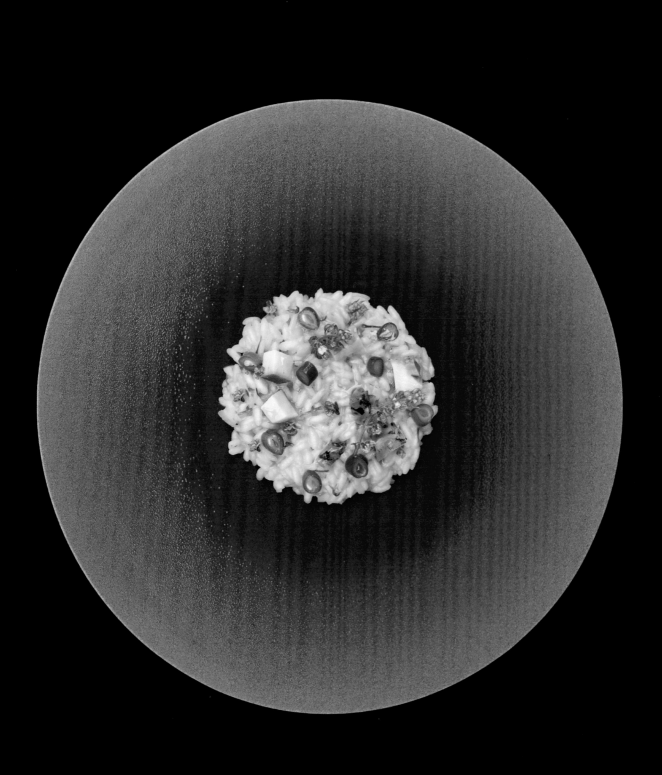

SAFFRON RISOTTO WITH ABALONE

I am often inspired by ingredients, but this time I was inspired by a plate. My Aritayaki ceramic plate strongly conveys an image of the blue sea. Although it is said that using a blue color in a restaurant decreases the appetite, I very much wanted a plate that made me think of the sea. I created my version of saffron risotto, which is famous in northern Italy, where I trained. I added abalone and abalone stock. While eating this dish, I would like diners to taste, see, and feel the sea.

1 young abalone in the shell, about 4 inches wide

Sea salt

1 quart bottled water, plus more as needed

2 tablespoons sake

1 tablespoon extra-virgin olive oil

1 small shallot, minced

¼ cup carnaroli rice

1 tablespoon white wine

10 saffron strands

3 tablespoons grated Grana Padano cheese

2 teaspoons unsalted butter

2 green beans, blanched and sliced ¼ inch thick, or 10 fresh peas, according to preference

Perilla leaves or Hojiso perilla flowers, for garnish if available

SERVES 2

Lightly sprinkle the abalone meat, still in the shell, with salt. Leave for about 20 minutes at room temperature to draw out some of the dirty water from the abalone. Wash under the faucet to further remove any debris.

Place the water and sake in a saucepan and bring to a gentle boil over low heat. Add the abalone, still in the shell, and cook for 1½ to 2 hours, until the abalone about as soft as the tip of your nose. If the water starts to completely evaporate, add some more. Transfer the abalone and cooking liquid to a bowl, let cool, then refrigerate overnight. There should be just under 1 cup of abalone stock.

The next day, remove the abalone from the shell with a spoon or spatula. It should separate easily, leaving the guts behind on the shell. Use a meat knife to cut the meat into ¼-inch cubes. Strain the stock through a fine-mesh sieve into a small saucepan and reheat until very hot. Keep on low.

In another pot, heat the olive oil and shallot in a pot over low heat for 1 minute, just to bring out the aromas. Add the rice and cook, stirring, just until toasted a bit, about 1 minute. Add the white wine and keep stirring until it is mostly absorbed, about 15 seconds. Add the saffron and stir into the rice. Continuing to stir, add some abalone stock, a little at a time, until each addition is absorbed, the risotto is creamy, and the grains of rice are soft on the outside but still al dente on the inside.

Add the Grana Padano, butter, and 1 teaspoon salt and stir until the butter and cheese melt and evenly coat the rice. Stir in most of the abalone and green beans, saving a few pieces of each for garnish, and season with salt if needed.

To serve, spoon the risotto onto bright blue plates, if you have them, and top with the reserved abalone and green bean pieces for decoration. Garnish with the perilla.

NOTE: You need to begin preparing the abalone one day in advance.

SHINSUKE
ISHII

SINCÈRE

CONVIVIALITY

INNER STRENGTH

Shinsuke Ishii extends his arms on a table at Sincère as he sits fiddling with a shred of paper, examining it with great focus as he speaks, searching for the right words. Head tilted, he recalls his childhood, when he delighted in cooking at home with his mother. Her tenderness and supportive demeanor in the kitchen sparked his future culinary career. He recounts dining out as a subdued experience when he and his siblings were required to be quiet and reserved at all times. He vowed to change this when he had his own family one day.

Sharing food the southern European way was one of the most significant and long-lasting memories of Ishii's time living in France. The notion that enjoying a long family meal could be gregarious and convivial for hours on end at a restaurant, and with children in tow, made an impact on Ishii, informing his cooking philosophy.

In addition to his mother, and his embrace of how meals are shared in France, Ishii discusses his profound reverence for the samurai. Samurai never gave up, and were always patient and consistent in their pursuit of a goal. Ishii simultaneously values the inner beauty and strength of the samurai, as well as the outgoing image more prevalent abroad. At his restaurant, Sincère, the forty-one-year-old combines the observant and quiet nature of many of Japan's best chefs with the outgoing and interactive repartee he enjoyed in France.

Sincère is located in Sendagaya, in a subterranean space with doors that open onto a small inner courtyard. The centerpiece of the polished yet informal dining room is the open kitchen—every seat in the house faces the action. Ishii's *omakase*-only (chef's choice) dinner starts with his version of oysters meunière presented atop rocks, finished with crisp seaweed and chrysanthemum. Next is a superconcentrated opening bite called Taste of Tomato. Tomato water is served in the form of a savory and airy white gelato with a peppery and sweet candylike tomato *tuile*, rosemary powder, and touch of sea salt. It is served in a Japanese cypress (*hinoki*) wood bowl, handmade specially for Ishii by a carpenter in Hachioji. But the dish most emblematic of Ishii's style is his savory tilefish *taiyaki*, a spin on a popular Japanese fish-shaped cake. His winsome pastry is golden and flaky and served in a swathe of cloth napkins. It is the perfect example of the playful and convivial side of Ishii, at the core of his life and cooking.

Why do you cook?

I was inspired by my mother. She's a hair stylist and worked out of our home. She was always so busy, so I needed to help her. My mother had a lot of cookbooks. In one there was a recipe for *choux* cream [a Japanese-style cream puff] that I tried to make, and my mom thought it was very tasty. I was fascinated by how the *choux* pastry rose. Everyone liked it, and this made me happy. I liked how everyone reacted to my making this pastry.

When I was older and went to France to live and work for a while, I noticed how families and friends enjoyed their food together so much. In Japan, people are much more quiet during a meal. We are taught to be reserved and proper. I like to create the French feeling of eating at Sincère.

What is your earliest memory?

American hot dogs. My mom used to make a lot of little American hot dogs, the tiny ones. Hot dogs are on my menu here, but I make them with boudin noir.

What motivates you?

The sense that I want to make my customers happy—service is so important. At the end of the day, I will be happy when they are, and if they're not, then I feel bad. But sometimes I have no way of knowing if they are happy or not, so I will think about what I could have done to be better. That will then motivate me to think about a new idea.

How do you think growing up in Japan informs your style?

I studied French food, but I definitely transmit the Japanese essence of *gochisou*, which basically means to serve food with great effort and lofty intention—it's an old word. It's a way of using seasonal food in a subtle way, preparing it with Japanese spirit, and serving it to the customer with attentive hospitality.

For you, what does it mean to be Japanese?

I love history and samurai. I wear a red apron that is inspired by the samurai Sanada Yukimura. A samurai is extremely loyal, honest, and modest, yet has strong ambition and desire to sacrifice everything to devote himself to the greater good.

I love Tokyo, where I am from, and I love Japan. When I went to live in France, I realized how reserved and shy the Japanese are and how we really don't talk a lot. I think this is actually nice; we have inner beauty and strength. We have strong feelings inside, even if we don't express them outwardly. Working with foreign chefs, I learned how they so freely express their feelings.

Why French food?

My dad likes sushi and told me to be a sushi chef, but I thought Western food would be cooler. I love Japan, but I just thought that food from overseas was cooler. I like French food. I have been cooking now for twenty years. The more I studied French food, the more profound it seemed; I liked it more and more. The small differences are interesting to me. I feel proud of myself cooking French food.

If you could share a meal with anyone, who would it be?

Samurai Sanada Yukimura.

What is your favorite word?

I would like to give you three: justice, morality, and honor.

What is one of your favorite films?

Gladiator with Russell Crowe. I like the theme of men and their strength, just as I like samurai.

TILEFISH TAIYAKI

Taiyaki is a sweet fish-shaped cake that's traditionally filled with red bean paste. I wanted to use French pastry in a Japanese style in this savory version of the dish. When I used my taiyaki pan to prepare it at home with puff pastry, it turned out very crispy and tasty. I thought it would be good idea to serve it at my restaurant.

PUFF PASTRY

¾ cup water

1 teaspoon salt

¾ cup plus 1 teaspoon bread flour

¾ cup plus 1 teaspoon cake flour

10 tablespoons cold unsalted butter

MOUSSE

4 ounces sea scallops

5½ ounces tilefish, diced

⅓ cup heavy cream

⅓ cup egg whites (about 2½ egg whites) plus 1 egg, lightly beaten

2 pinches of sea salt

Pinch of cayenne powder

SERVES 6

To prepare the puff pastry, stir together the water and salt in a small bowl. In a large bowl, stir together the bread flour and cake flour. Pour the salted water into the flour mixture and mix with your hands until the dough becomes smooth. Transfer the dough to a floured work surface and gather it into a ball. Place the dough in a bowl, cover with plastic wrap, and let it rest overnight in the refrigerator.

The next morning, roll out the dough on a floured surface to a 6-inch square that is ⅛ inch thick. Knead the cold butter into one brick, then roll and flatten it with the rolling pin to a 5-inch square that is about ¼ inch thick. If needed, chill the butter again so it is very cold.

Place the butter on top of the dough on the diagonal, and wrap the dough over the butter, folding the corners in from each side. Next, fold the dough into thirds like a business letter. Repeat this three times. Wrap the dough in plastic wrap and refrigerate overnight.

The next morning, on a floured surface, roll out the dough to a 20 by 15-inch rectangle that is ⅛ inch thick. Cut the dough into twelve 5 by 3-inch rectangles. (Wrap and freeze the remaining dough for another use.) Place the pastry rectangles on a parchment paper–lined baking sheet and refrigerate until ready to use.

To make the mousse, place the scallops and 4 ounces of the tilefish in a food processor and process until the mixture is smooth, 20 to 30 seconds. Add the cream. Mix for 5 seconds. Add the egg whites, salt, and cayenne and mix again until incorporated, about 5 seconds more.

To assemble the *taiyaki*, place a pastry rectangle on a work surface. Place one piece of the remaining diced tilefish in the center. Add 2 teaspoons of mousse on top of the tilefish. Cover with another piece of pastry. With your fingers, lightly press the edges together so that the mixture does not seep through. Brush the top of the pastry with the beaten egg. Repeat to make five more *taiyaki*.

Place one or two *taiyaki* in the *taiyaki* pan (which does not need to be oiled) and cook until golden brown, about 10 minutes. Repeat with the remaining pastries. Serve immediately.

NOTE: A *taiyaki* pan is required for this recipe. It is similar to a nonstick, stove-top waffle pan but with a fish-shaped design. They are available online. You need to start the puff pastry two days in advance. Or, you can use store-bought puff pastry instead of making it yourself. You will have leftover puff pastry and you may have some extra mousse.

DAISUKE
KANEKO

L'AS

EFFICIENCY

SPEED

Daisuke Kaneko is practical and often in a hurry. He tells me that he likes simplicity and came to the culinary world not because he had a strong calling but because it was sensible. After seeing a video about cooking in high school, he decided this was a good choice and he stuck with it. He worked at the famed Senderens in Paris as a *grillardin* in charge of the meat station and, like many of his colleagues, he was changed by his time living abroad. Kaneko, thirty-eight, likes the direct style of European communication better, especially in the kitchen where he prefers that things move along briskly.

Sitting at a table in L'As (Ace in English) essentially means sitting in the kitchen. The entrance leads diners directly into it. The restaurant is one open rectangular space, without a counter. This open floor plan allows diners to immerse themselves in vigorous culinary creativity and action.

Above the island is a prominent multicolored chandelier of round, glass baubles. Along the far wall are mirrors, giving the kitchen the illusion that it is wider than it is. Kaneko's wife, Tae, comes out to greet me in French. The kitchen is filled with quite a large crew; some are chefs and some are servers, but they overlap in many of their responsibilities. Kaneko has a rapid style of plating, in line with his preference for alacrity. His trademark is painterly syncopated gestures, smears, splotches, zigzags, and graphic patterns. He wants to present the dish, like his Hungarian duckling with pipérade sauce and couscous, to his diners as soon as possible, anticipating the satisfaction and reward of watching them enjoy his food.

What Kaneko has created here is not French food. His food certainly incorporates French cooking technique, but his combinations and dishes are too eclectic and far off the scale of French to classify it as such. Kaneko also has an efficient deli restaurant called Recipe + Market at Tokyo Midtown in Roppongi, where he spends time between services at L'As. As I leave after lunch, both Tae and Kaneko follow me out for a brief goodbye, before Kaneko must jump on his motor bike and zip over to Roppongi. He does not have much time; speed is important.

INTER VIEW

Why do you cook?

There's no reason really. Cooking is nothing special for me. I like cooking. I like having a team. I like working. It is the first career I started, and I continued with it.

It's easy to see the outcome when you cook. You can see right away whether or not the customer is happy. The process is quick and easy to see, and you get satisfaction. I like speed. I'm a bit impatient in general.

What was your experience like in France?

I was scared at first. I couldn't speak French. I couldn't speak anything but Japanese. In France, people are direct and straightforward. I like it; I think it's easier. Before going to France, I thought French technique would be better. But now I think some Japanese techniques are better, some not. It's mixed.

Working at Senderens, I learned some modern techniques from chef Alain Senderens and a system for cooking; I learned to communicate and be more direct. I missed Japan, the organization. It's comfortable here; you can predict how things will work. Things are on time. Precision and exactness are great. But for creativity, France is better.

For you, what does it mean to be Japanese?

I can do everything precisely, I am organized. I never break a promise.

Why did you decide on your restaurant design?

I wanted an open kitchen because it's easier to serve, it's very functional. I want to see the customers' faces. If you can't, it's boring. Here, chefs also serve what they've made. I like simplicity. I don't like a lot of decoration. I like minimalism.

Who had the biggest influence on your cooking?

My mom actually, chef Masao Saisu of Cote D'Or, chef Alain Senderens, and Yoshinori Shibuya of La Bécasse.

What is your earliest food memory?

My mother cooked well when I was growing up in Hiroshima. I sometimes went to my friend's houses to eat, but my mother's cooking was always better. She made amazing birthday cakes. She baked bread from scratch. She made Chinese, Japanese, and European foods. She also made delicious *nagashi somen* [very fine wheat noodles]. We had that often.

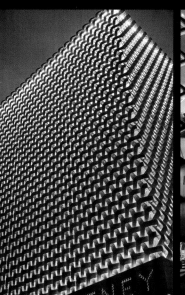

SALTED TUNA WITH BEETS AND OLIVES

The most important thing for my recipes is to focus on the flavor of ingredients first, then the color and presentation. I create my menus by combining tastes and textures inspired by the very essence of the ingredients themselves, rather than any external or abstract ideas or concepts.

3 ounces beets, peeled

Sea salt

1 tablespoon pitted black olives (packed in water, not olive oil), plus 1 tablespoon of the water the olives came in

5½ ounces mebachi maguro (bigeye tuna)

1 or 2 pinches of fleur de sel

½ teaspoon extra-virgin olive oil

SERVES 2

Preheat the oven to 350°F.

Wrap the beets in aluminum foil. Bake until they become rather soft when pierced with a knife, about 90 minutes. Pour off any juices and let cool. Put the beets and olive water in a blender and puree until smooth. Season with about ¼ teaspoon sea salt and pulse again to combine.

Lightly cover the tuna with sea salt and place in a container with a flat bottom. Cover with plastic wrap and refrigerate for 15 minutes. Remove from the refrigerator and dab both sides with a paper towel to remove any excess moisture. Cut into ¾-inch slices.

Dry the black olives by placing them on a plate and then microwaving for 2 minutes. Let them rest for 1 minute. Repeat microwaving three to five more times until very dry. Place the dried olives in a blender and pulse for 10 seconds to pulverize them to a powder. If you have a high-speed blender, set it to grind.

To serve, place the beet puree on a serving plate in a design with a knife or spoon and sprinkle with the olive powder. Place the tuna on top of the beet puree, sprinkle with the fleur de sel, and drizzle with olive oil.

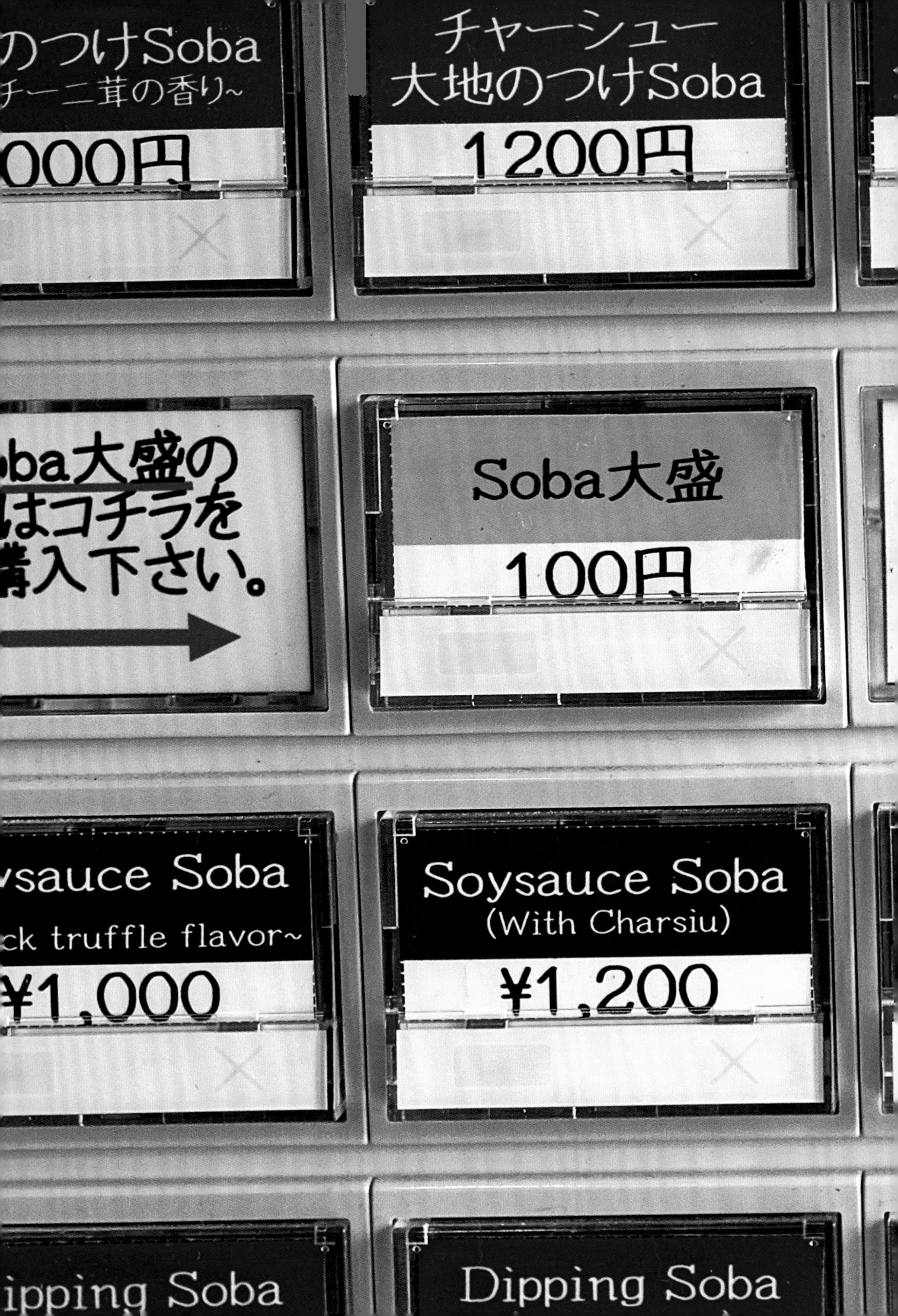

のつけSoba
チーニ茸の香り~
000円
チャーシュー
大地のつけSoba
1200円
oba大盛の
はコチラを
入下さい。
Soba大盛
100円
ysauce Soba
ck truffle flavor~
¥1,000
Soysauce Soba
(With Charsiu)
¥1,200
ipping Soba
Dipping Soba

ワンタン
地のつけSoba
1300円

チャーシューワンタン
大地のつけSoba
1500円

ッピングは
コチラを
購入下さい。→

ワンタン
（純血在来種アグー豚）
300円

YUKI
ONISHI

oysauce Soba
(With Wonton)
¥1,300

Soysauce Soba
(With Charsiu&Wonton)
¥1,500

JAPANESE
SOBA NOODLES
TSUTA

Dipping Soba

Dipping Soba

CONFIDENCE

REINVENTION

Like many people, I cannot eat ramen without thinking about Juzo Itami's legendary film *Tampopo*, one of the most original and magical films ever made about food and the quest for perfection. The joy, quirkiness, humor, and intensity of it all—in reverence to the perfect bowl of broth, noodles, and pork—was one of my first introductions to Japan. The film is the story of Tampopo, a hardworking mother and owner of a struggling ramen shop. With the help of a discerning cowboy trucker, she sets out on a quest for ramen perfection.

To eat at Yuki Onishi's ramen shop, Japanese Soba Noodles Tsuta, it is essential to plan in advance. There is a ticket system in place ever since Onishi received a Michelin star; massive crowds line up daily so this system was necessary. Tsuta is not open late, just for lunch from eleven to four. Right inside the entrance stands the classic vending machine with which the ramen is chosen and prepurchased.

Onishi's uniform is a white T-shirt and navy blue cotton jacket. I spot gold 7 and 9 charms dangling from a chain around his neck, 1979 being the year of his birth. He is stoic and measured as he prepares shoyu ramen for me. It contains *yakibuta* (roast sliced pork loin), *nibuta* (braised pork belly), *hosaki menma* (a condiment made from bamboo shoots), enoki mushrooms, Japanese leek, *kujo negi* (Japanese green onions), melted chicken fat, Italian black truffle oil, and a potent housemade black truffle sauce. The noodles contain three kinds of wheat: *yumechikara* and *kitahonami* from Hokkaido, and *iwainodaichi* from Tochigi. With an intense amount of umami, the taste and smell of my bowl of ramen lingers. The pork stands out; it is distinct from many ramen shops' in texture and flavor. Cut in thin slices and braised, it is soft and full flavored rather than firm and bland. I ask Onishi where it is from, but he declines to answer. It is a secret.

On a trip to Kappabashi (a famous Tokyo street of kitchen and restaurant supply shops) together, Onishi reveals that his father was a ramen chef. Onishi worked at his ramen shop during high school, before tiring of it and pivoting to a career in fashion. After a few years, he had an epiphany and ramen lured him back to what he had always known. This time Onishi began studying ramen, setting out to formulate an extraordinary sauce that would be the key to distinguishing his from all the others. It worked. Onishi is making a bit of gastronomic history in an insatiable ramen-obsessed world.

INTERVIEW

Why do you cook?

My father had a ramen shop when I was in high school. At the time I had nothing much to do after school, and I would help him. I would cook and do just about everything.

What did you do after working with your father?

I delivered newspapers for two years and then decided to be a salesman in fashion. I traveled abroad working for Betsey Johnson and a couple of smaller names for four years. I went to New York City, Las Vegas, and Los Angeles for fashion exhibitions. I ate out a lot when traveling, and I started noticing the importance of sauce, and that stock was not important there. Traveling like this, I started thinking I might work in the food world again.

Why did you go back to ramen?

I chose to return to ramen because I wanted to make something where the dashi [stock] is important. This is the most important and essential part of Japanese cuisine. I was so focused and wanted to create something better than my father's. I also wanted to create a new, unique sauce.

What makes a great bowl of ramen?

Bringing out the flavor of each ingredient is the most important thing. I am trying to create layers of umami and of aroma. Umami has different directions, too, as well as different layers. There are three parts to umami, amino acid, *kaku* [nuoleic] acid, and *yuki* [organic] acid. There is the kombu, which contains amino acid, which in turn contains glutamic acid. There is the chicken and dry fish, which contains inosinic acid (which comes from nuoleic acid). There are the clams, which contain succinic acid. I layer these umami flavors to make my own umami flavor in my stock.

Umami runs lengthwise but also widthwise. Then there is also the taste and all the aftertastes. My sauce is also very important. It is different.

What is your earliest food memory when you were a little boy?

Pudding. My mother's friend's son had an Italian restaurant, and they served pudding. It was very shocking to me. It was like custard. The taste was great.

What does your Michelin star mean to you?

I don't need it, but it's nice to have.

Who do you admire in the food world?

Two legends who are gone now: Minoru Sano from Shinasoba-ya in Kanagawa, and Kazuo Yamagishi from Taisho-ken in Higashi Ikebukuro.

For you, what does it mean to be Japanese?

I grew up in Fujisawa City and am proud of myself as a Japanese. I think that dashi is only something that a Japanese person can make. It brings out all the flavors of all the other ingredients. The first person who discovered dashi was amazing.

If you could share a meal with anyone, who would it be?

Three of myself at different ages, maybe at thirty, fifty, and sixty. I'm nearly forty right now. I want to know my ideas at all these ages. I want to learn from myself and cook more delicious food.

What is your favorite word?

Kakugo, which means conviction.

What are your favorite films?

Cinema Paradiso for the human drama. *Chef* for the story of cooking, the insight into the chef's conviction, and his love for what he does.

醤油Soba 1000円
〜黒トリュフの香り〜

塩Soba 1000円
〜白トリュフの香り〜

由Soba ⧸ュフの香り〜 ⧸00円	チャーシュー醤油Soba 1200円	ワンタン醤油Soba 1300円	チャーシューワンタン 醤油Soba 1500円
つけSoba 〜二荒の香り〜 ⧸00円	チャーシュー 大地のつけSoba 1200円	ワンタン 大地のつけSoba 1300円	チャーシューワンタン 大地のつけSoba 1500円
ba大盛の コチラを 入下さい。 →	Soba大盛 100円	トッピングは コチラを ご購入下さい。 →	ワンタン (純血在来種アグー豚) 300円
auce Soba truffle flavor〜 1,000	Soysauce Soba (With Charsiu) ¥1,200	Soysauce Soba (With Wonton) ¥1,300	Soysauce Soba (With Charsiu&Wonton) ¥1,500
ping Soba u porcini flavor〜 1,000	Dipping Soba (With Chasiu) ¥1,200	Dipping Soba (With Wonton) ¥1,300	Dipping Soba (With Chasiu&Wonton) ¥1,500

Japanese Soba Noo

JINNOSUKE
UMEHARA

YAKUMO
SARYO

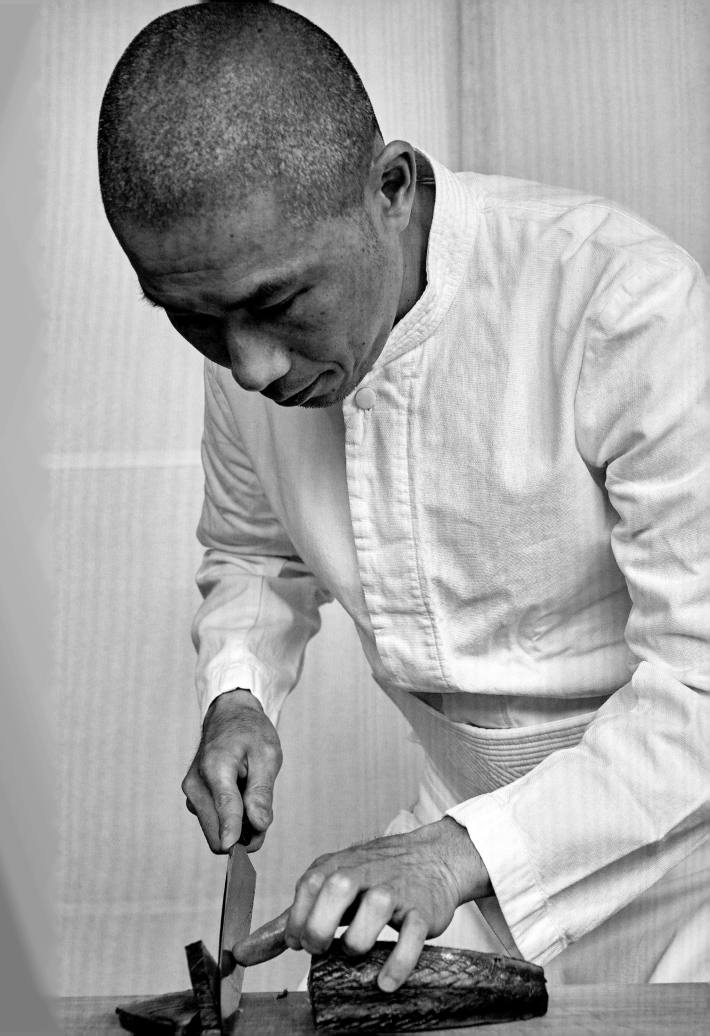

DESIGN

SIMPLICITY

Just outside the city center, tucked away in the a residential neighborhood of Meguro-ku, is an oasis of pure and modern Japanese style. To enter Yakumo Saryo is to step into a tranquil world where the spirit of the elements and the intent behind each object, ingredient, and gesture is full of meaning. Here, through his thoughtful design, owner and design director Shinichiro Ogata has created an elegant, contemporary, and personal homage to the essence of Japanese culture.

At the entrance, the large *noren* (traditional hanging fabric outside a restaurant or shop displaying the restaurant logo or name) billows ever so slightly in the wind, and just beyond it, the serene, minimalist space that is Yakumo Saryo feels like a sanctuary. Natural light drenches this former residence, which is composed mostly of stone, wood, glass, and concrete. There is an exquisite tearoom, a sweets shop featuring enticingly chic confections, a dining area with huge picture windows, and a spare but imposing open kitchen.

The head chef in the kitchen is Jinnosuke Umehara, a disciple of Ogata's. A native of Oita Prefecture on Kyushu, Japan's southernmost island, Umehara grew up in the countryside, a setting that had a profound influence on his outlook and approach to cooking. Clad in crisp, bright white from head to toe, including his *zori* (traditional Japanese style flip-flops), he is keen to share his love and knowledge of Japanese cooking and its inherent simplicity.

Dishes at Yakumo Saryo are created to express the energy of Shintoism and the belief that eight million gods live within every living creature. "As a chef, I am an artisan, not an artist," Umehara asserts. "I respect nature very much and want to celebrate and express the essence and soul of everything I prepare." One dish that clearly communicates this very message is the young *ayu* with *tade* (smartweed) tea served for lunch during one of my visits. The spartan, breathtaking presentation is both an affirmation of the significance of nature and a depiction of the profound essential beauty that is Japan. This cleanest and most crisp of dishes celebrates the precious *ayu* (sweetfish) swimming in the river, and the fresh, cool wild grasses and plants that grow nearby. It is a transporting dish of poetic purity and simplicity that exalts the intrinsic spirit of a nation.

INTERVIEW

Why do you cook?

My dad owns an *izakaya*, so I grew up in the food world. Also, in Oita, there is a strong ceramics and wood artisan presence. At first, I wanted to be a woodworking artist or ceramist. I thought it would be great to express feelings through food, however. Being a chef, I can still work with ceramics; I love making them.

What do you strive to express through your food?

So much has been handed down for many generations; we want to communicate this old wisdom and aesthetic of Japan. This can be found in Shinto beliefs, the essence of Japanese style, and includes the artisans, farmers, animals, and produce that all contribute to the meal I prepare each day at Yakumo Saryo. Everything is natural and pure. Preparing food is the worship of eight million gods. It is the worship of water, air, and sunlight. I really believe that the foods have power from nature and spirit. I want to pass this spirit on to our guests. Ogata is redefining what Japanese food should be now. It is contemporary Japanese food.

What motivates you every morning?

How to express the work of the farmers and fishermen and all the people behind the production of the food. I want to do well by them.

What is your earliest food memory?

On my grandmother's farm, when she was cooking taro. She would harvest and grill them. Before tasting my grandmother's taros, I didn't like them. Then I loved them! They were very tasty because they were grilled with leaves. And they were so aromatic.

For you, what does it mean to be Japanese?

I'm not religious, but I believe in Shintoism and eight million gods. I respect nature a lot; that comes from Shintoism. This also comes from me growing up in the countryside in Kyushu. My grandfather was a carpenter for traditional buildings and shrines. For me as a child, carving wood calmed me and brought me clarity. Although I believe that people from other countries have similar spirit, Japan is an island country. We found our own unique way of living with the elements here.

What do you like most about Tokyo?

I like the diverse cultures of Tokyo, starting from the samurai culture, which goes back to the Kamakura era, as well as the structure of public culture of the Edo era, which still influences the culture today. The duality of chaos and cosmos is what makes Tokyo different from other cities and countries.

If you could share a meal with anyone, who would it be?

Takeshi Kaiko [writer].

Takashi Nakazato [ceramist].

Naomichi Ishige [cultural anthropologist].

What is your favorite word?

Ichizu, which means one direction, one way, one thing.

What is one of your favorite films?

A River Runs Through It. It gives me joy to discover a beautiful river. I grew up with a river nearby, and throughout my childhood and adolescent years, I learned a lot of things from the river and fishing in it. I find beauty in how the film captures the harmonious relationship between nature and men.

CHARGRILLED YOUNG AYU WITH TADE TEA

The cedarwood grain of the hassun (tray), on which the ayu (sweetfish) is plated, is likened to the stream of a river, and tade (smartweed) tea is likened to the aroma of the grass that grows by the river. Traditionally, the fish is served with cold-brewed Karigane.

6 tablespoons Karigane tea

3⅓ cups cold, filtered water

Salt

4 young ayu (sweetfish) or small trout, each 5 to 6 inches long, scaled with the back of a knife and washed

12 tade leaves

SERVES 2

Combine the loose tea and filtered water in a covered pitcher and let sit at room temperature for 8 hours.

Lightly salt the ayu. Preheat and oil a charcoal grill to medium-high heat. Put the fish on a metal skewer from head to tail, bending the fish in the middle. The fish should form an S shape. Place the head end of the fish closest to the hottest part of the grill and the tail away from the hottest part. Cover the grill. Grill until the head is crispy and the rest of the fish is soft, 15 to 20 minutes. Test for doneness with a fork at the thickest part of the fish.

Grind 10 of the tade leaves with a mortar and pestle and add 2 cups of the cold-brewed tea. Stir lightly and strain through a fine-mesh sieve into two chilled glasses. Add a whole tade leaf to each glass for presentation. Place each glass along with the ayu on a *hassun* (tray) for serving.

NOTE: *Tade* is a bitter green cress that grows by the river and is traditionally served with *ayu*. If you can't find *tade*, use another type of cress. The fish are grilled and eaten whole, but if you do not prefer to eat the innards, you can have your fishmonger gut the fish. Karigane tea is a green tea made from Gyokuro and Sencha.

TOKYO RESTAURANT GUIDE

Abysse / Chef Kotaro Meguro
Aoyama TMI 1st Floor
4-9-9, Minami-Aoyama, Minato-ku
information@abysse.jp
abysse.jp/en

Anis / Chef Susumu Shimizu
1-9-7 Hatsudai, Shibuya-ku
Tel: +81 3-6276-0026
restaurant-anis.jp
*Fluency in Japanese is required to
make reservations.*

Äta / Chef Satoshi Kakegawa
1F, 2-5 Sarugakucho, Shibuya-ku
info@ata1789.com
ata1789.com
*Fluency in Japanese is required to
make reservations.*

Convivio / Chef Daisuke Tsuji
Kamimura Building 1st Floor
3-17-12 Sendagaya, Shibuya-ku
Tel: +81 50-5570-4441
convivio.jp
*Fluency in Japanese is required to
make reservations.*

Craftale / Chef Shinya Otsuchihashi
2F 1-16-11 Aobadai, Meguro-ku
Tel: +81 3-6277-5813
tables.jp.net/craftale
*Fluency in Japanese is required to
make reservations.*

Den / Chef Zaiyu Hasegawa
Architect House Hall JIA
2-3-18 Jingumae, Shibuya-ku
Tel: +81 3-6455-5433
jimbochoden.com/en

**Erba da Nakahigashi /
Chef Toshifumi Nakahigashi**
Nishi-Azabu 4416 Building B1F
4-4-16 Nishi-Azabu, Minato-ku
erbadanakahigashi.com
Make reservations online.

Esquisse / Chef Lionel Beccat
Royal Crystal Building Ginza 9th Floor
5-4-6 Ginza, Chuo-ku
Tel: +81 3-5537-5580
esquissetokyo.com

Florilège / Chef Hiroyasu Kawate
Seizan Gaienmae B1F
2-5-4 Jingumae, Shibuya-ku
florilege@aoyama-florilege.jp
aoyama-florilege.jp/en

Kamachiku / Chef Yoshihiro Hiraoka
2-14-18 Nezu, Bunky-ku
kamachiku.com
No reservation required, but no English spoken.

Kohaku / Chef Koji Koizumi
3-4 Kagurazaka, Shinjuku-ku
Tel: +81 3-5225-0807

L'As / Chef Daisuke Kaneko
Minamiaoyama Kotori Building
4-16-3 Minamiaoyama, Minato-ku
Tel: +81 80-3310-4058
las-minamiaoyama.com/index
Fluency in Japanese is required to make reservations.

L'Effervescence / Chef Shinobu Namae
2-26-4 Nishiazabu, Minato-ku
leffervescence.jp/en
Make reservations online.

Ode / Chef Yusuke Namai
2F 5-1-32 Hiroo, Shibuya-ku
info@restaurant-ode.com
restaurant-ode.com

Organ / Chef Makoto Konno
2 Chome-19-12 Nishiogiminami
Suginami-ku
Tel: +81 3-5941-5388

Owan / Chef Kuniatsu Kondo
Okada Building 1st Floor
2-26-7 Ikejiri, Setagaya-ku
Tel: +81 3-5486-3844
owan-tokyo.com
Fluency in Japanese is required to make reservations.

Pellegrino / Chef Hayato Takahashi
2-3-4 Ebisu, Shibuya-ku
Tel: +81 3-6277-4697
pellegrino.jp
Fluency in Japanese is required to make reservations about eight months in advance.

Quintessence / Chef Shuzo Kishida
Shinagawa Gotenyama 1F
6-7-29 Garden City, Kitashinagawa
Shinagawa-ku
Tel: +81 3-6277-0090
quintessence.jp/index
Reservations by telephone only.

Salmon & Trout / Chef Kan Morieda
4-42-7 Daizawa, Setagaya-ku
Tel: +81 80-4816-1831

Sincère / Chef Shinsuke Ishii
Harajuku Tokyo Apartment B1
3-7-13 Sendagaya, Shibuya-ku
Tel: +81 3-6804-2006
Fluency in Japanese is required to make reservations.

Sugalabo / Chef Yosuke Suga
sugalabo.com
By referral only.

Sugita / Chef Takaaki Sugita
View Heights Building B1F
1-33-6, Kakigara-cho, Nihonbashi,
Chuo-ku
Tel: +81 3-3669-3855
Fluency in Japanese is required to make reservations about eight months in advance.

Sumibiyakiniku Nakahara / Chef Kentaro Nakahara
GEMS Building Ichigaya 9th Floor
4-3 Rokubancho, Chiyoda-ku
Tel: +81 3-6261-2987
sumibiyakinikunakahara.com/sp/en

Sushi Take / Chef Fumie Takeuchi
Ishii Kishuya Building 4th Floor
7-6-5 Ginza Chuo-ku
Tel: +81 3-6228-5007
Fluency in Japanese is required to make reservations.

Sushi Tokami / Chef Hiroyuki Sato*
Ginza Seiwa Silver Building B1F
8-2-10 Ginza, Chup-Ku
Tel: +81 3-3571-6005
sushi-tokami.com
*As of this book's printing, Hiroyuki Sato has left Sushi Tokami with plans to open another sushi restaurant.

Sushiya / Chef Takao Ishiyama
6-3-17 Ginza, Chuo-ku
Tel: +81 3-3571-7900
Fluency in Japanese is required to make reservations.

Takazawa / Chef Yoshiaki Takazawa
3-5-2 Akasaka, Minato-ku
reservation@takazawa-y.co.jp
takazawa-y.co.jp/en

Torishiki / Chef Yoshiteru Ikegawa
2-14-12 Kamiosaki, Shinagawa-ku
Tel: +81 3-3440-7656
Fluency in Japanese is required to make reservations.

Yakumo Saryo / Chef Jinnosuke Umehara
3-4-7 Yakumo, Meguro-ku
yakumosaryo.jp/e
Dinner by referral only. Reservations available for breakfast and lunch without referral.

House / Chef Yuji Tani
Nishiazabu Showcase 4th Floor
2-24-7 Nishiazabu, Minato-ku
housestaub.jp
Make reservations online.

Japanese Soba Noodles Tsuta / Chef Yuki Onishi
Plateau-Saka 1st Floor
1 Chome-14-1 Sugamo, Toshima-ku
For a refundable deposit, tickets are distributed outside the restaurant starting at 7 a.m. The ticket represents a seating time at which you can return to the restaurant that same day to eat.

ABOUT THE AUTHOR

CYNTHIA WIMER

ANDREA FAZZARI is a Tokyo-based international photographer, author, stylist, and dining consultant specializing in travel and the culinary world. *Tokyo New Wave* is Andrea's love letter to Japan and its distinct philosophy and approach to food. She is an insider in the city's food scene, working regularly with Tokyo's many influential and respected chefs.

Andrea is the photographer and stylist of *Aperitivo*, shot entirely on location in Italy. She is Starwood Hotels and Resorts' first Luxury Collection Global Explorer; her photographs, journal entries, and audio narration of her travels on six continents are featured on the Luxury Collection website and in the *Luxury Collection Destination Guides*. She is a tastemaker in *Hotel Stories*, a travel book that showcases unique luxury properties around the world, and is the featured photographer for the book *BVLGARI La Cucina di Luca Fantin*, photographed in Japan.

Andrea is the recipient of the Lowell Thomas Gold Award for travel photography. She photographs campaigns and projects for such companies as Cathay Pacific Airlines and Four Seasons Hotels, and magazines from *Travel + Leisure* and *Vanity Fair* to *Architectural Digest* and *Departures*. *Four* magazine has profiled Andrea and her culinary work, and *Photo District News* featured her as one of the year's best cookbook photographers in their food issue for 2017.

In addition to Tokyo and her native Manhattan, Andrea has lived in Paris, Florence, and Hong Kong. She speaks English, Italian, French, and Spanish. In 2004, she was named one of *Photo District News*' "30 New and Emerging Photographers to Watch." She became a photographer by chance after working in fashion and film public relations for Giorgio Armani, Dolce & Gabbana, and Miramax Films.

Visit her at AndreaFazzari.com or on Instagram at Tokyo_New_Wave.

INDEX